# Just Ask MOM

# Just Ask MM

Everything she told you when you weren't listening is in this book.

**NANCY MALONE, M.O.M.**

**C P O**
**PUBLISHING**
a WAYNICK BOOK GROUP Co.

Franklin, Tennessee

Published by CPO Publishing
A Waynick Book Group Company
101 Forrest Crossing Boulevard
Suite 100
Franklin, Tennessee 37064
(615) 277–5555

ISBN-13: 978-1-93431-432-6
ISBN-10: 1-93431-432-3

First Printing 2008
Printed in the United States of America
10 9 8 7 6 5 4 3 2 1

Managing Editor: Shannon Whitehead
Art Director: Marc Pewitt
Illustrator: Duane Gillogly, Publication Services, Inc.; Jupiter Images

# TABLE OF CONTENTS

Be ready to improvise. (Emergency Substitutions!)
Learn to appreciate our friend, vinegar.
Utilize your microwave.
Enjoy grilling and/or barbequing.
Remember the green stuff!

First things first: Plan ahead.
Gather your serving essentials.
Set that table.
Realize that buffets are not just for Chinese restaurants!
Be a good host/hostess.
Be a good neighbor, too.
Consider having a theme for your gathering.

Start with the starters.
Better make some beverages.
Bring on the breakfast!
Serve some savory salads.
Soothe (and satisfy) with soups.
Serve sizzlin' sandwiches.
Serve delicious sides.
Master memory-making main dishes.
Dazzle with desserts!
Fix something festive!

First things first: Budget, budget, budget!
Don't spend more than you earn—or as Mom says: Live within
   your means.
Be frugal.
Pay with cash.
BE VERY CAREFUL with credit cards.
Balance your checkbook.
Utilize online and fee-free banking.
Go ahead and buy the insurance.
Save for a rainy day.
Pay your bills on time and establish a good credit rating.
Know the difference between a "need" and a "want"—and don't
   want everything you see!
Search for good values and find deals.
Cut back at home and save some cash.
REALITY CHECK: Don't borrow from your family & friends, and
   don't loan money to family & friends.
Be like the Magi: give gifts wisely.
Make it a priority to donate and to tithe to your church.
Know how to tip.

Last but not least: File your tax returns on time!

First things first: By all means, groom yourself.
Embrace your own style.
Dress appropriately for appointments and events.
Be able to tie a tie.

First things first: Know what makes relationships succeed.
Be open to friendship.
Choose friends who are good for (and to) you.
Be a good listener. (Don't talk too much!)
Take the time to remember names.
If you can't say anything nice, don't say anything at all.
See the value in everyone.
Dating: Remember the possibilities.
Be creative when dating.
Know who's getting the bill.
Be a grateful date.
Show maturity with your cell phone (the relationship connector).
Roommates: Handle with care.
Be choosy.
Set some house rules.
Address problems calmly and quickly.
Last, but certainly not least: Kindness counts.

First things first: Live by basic safety rules.
Keep your home secure.
Keep your automobile safe and running well.
Follow bike safety.
Be vigilant on walks or runs.
Be prepared for emergencies.

First things first: Pack a first aid kit.
Know how to alleviate common ailments and illnesses.
Know about serious and chronic illnesses.
Deal with in-your-face issues.
Beware of STDs.
Avoid drug and alcohol use and abuse.
Get smart about smoking and tobacco use.
Eat well.
Make time to exercise.
Get plenty of sleep.

# DEDICATION

*For Elizabeth, Will, Roger, and Katie*

*I am so thankful that I have had
the opportunity to be your Mom.*

*I can't imagine what my life
would have been like without you.*

# ACKNOWLEDGEMENTS

When you are a young person, you always think, "Oh, I won't need to know that." Guess what—we all need to know all those little bits of information that someone took the time to teach us. As I jotted down the various parts of this book, my mind flooded with memories of time spent with my own Mom, my grandmothers, and all the women who have taught me so much over the years.

Those blessed memories have made writing this a labor of love.

When I began writing, my oldest child was a freshman in college. I tried to think of all the things that I would want her to know, as well as my other children. I was also lucky enough to receive countless phone calls from her with those first-year-away-from-home types of questions; the answers to those questions and more can be found in these pages. I also tried to think back to the days when I first lived on my own, and what I didn't know back then.

I have been encouraged and cheered on by many people during the process of writing this book, and I am eternally grateful for the support. I am especially thankful to my husband, Roger. You always said I could do it, and I thank you for not giving up on me when I procrastinated. I am blessed and honored to have you by my side as my partner. I am also thankful to my children, Elizabeth, Will, Roger, and Katie, for having patience with me as I completed this endeavor. You guys were real troopers when I was closed up in the library typing away on my computer. Thanks for not being too frustrated with me when I said, "Only two more pages tonight." I love you five people more than anything in the world.

I wish to thank all the great people at Waynick Book Group and CPO Publishing for having faith in me and giving me this opportunity: Carol Pierce Olson, my publisher; Cindy Games, project manager; and Marc Pewitt, designer. I owe a huge thanks to my editor, Shannon Whitehead, who was a delight and pleasure to work with.

Last, and certainly not least, I wish to thank and recognize all the Moms who have taught me so much over the years. From you, I learned to cook, to clean, to take care of children, to repair things that are broken, and to patch up skinned knees. By watching many of you, I also learned how to treat other people and how to love my family. Some of these lovely ladies are no longer with us, but they have certainly lived in my thoughts as I shared the lessons they taught me. I hope I have made you all proud: my mother, Helen Malone; my grandmothers, Irene Foutch and Nonnie Malone; my mother-in-law, June Waynick; my aunts, Harriett Cantrell, Alma Dean Henley, Norma Malone, Roberta Robinson, Ann Campbell, Mainell Foutch, and Patty Malone; my great-aunt Opal Hurst; my aunt by marriage, Peggy Sipes; and my dear friends and mentors, Delia Mae Cripps, Marie Colvert, and Minnie Lee Walker. I am grateful to you all.

# INTRODUCTION

Moms only have a few years to teach our children all the basics of life, and in between soccer practice, piano lessons, and incidental interruptions—not to mention the quick passing of time—some important lessons just don't get discussed. Others are talked over, but quickly forgotten. (How important is boiling an egg, hemming a skirt, or tying a necktie to a fifteen-year-old?!)

In case you or anyone you know needs a refresher course on how to do some of life's basic requirements, *Just Ask Mom* is here, a handbook with instructions for all the things a young person will need to know to live life on their own.

Even for those who embark on adulthood feeling well-equipped, *Just Ask Mom* serves as a helpful tool for those times that you need a little assistance. After all, everyone can't be good at everything every day, so when you forget how to perform a task (or never knew you'd need to know how to in the first place), perhaps you can find the answers here.

In this friendly, low-key manual, you can find answers about cleaning, cooking, managing your money, applying first aid, entertaining your friends, and even sewing on a button—all written with the tender, loving humor of Mom.

Fortunately, Moms don't mind being asked, "Now how do you do that again?" After all, we've become experts on a variety of subjects. We have taken care of helpless babies, nursed the sick, and tucked in the sleepy. We've read to both attentive and squirmy audiences, picked up after human tornadoes, cooked for finicky palates, and bought both necessities and unnecessary "fun stuff." We've encouraged, scolded, yelled at, sang to, prayed for, and driven around our kids and their friends, and stayed up too many nights waiting to hear that car with its precious cargo pull into the driveway.

Through the hustle and bustle, we've done our best to pass along what we know, preparing for that day when we'll send our children out into the world to live on their own.

Just in case you've forgotten some of those maternal tidbits of wisdom and practicality, this book's for you.

Love,
Mom

**P.S.** You would think that, with all the hours logged and expertise accumulated, Moms would be entitled to a salary equivalent to the most well paid CEO. But the truth is that most Moms would happily settle for a heartfelt thank you or a simple hug.

# CHAPTER ONE

# Let's Get Organized!

*"It is easier to keep up than to catch up."*

How true this saying is. Although it may sound a bit obsessive-compulsive, life really is easier when you are organized. Creating organizing systems and discovering ways to stay on top of all areas of your life are essential to keeping life's chaos at bay. If you just take the time to set up some systems to help you keep your appointments, deal with mail, pay your bills, and keep up with daily tasks, you will feel empowered. Being organized really just means you have found some good ways to simplify your everyday life.

Of course, each one of us is unique, so when you organize your schedule, put your individual priorities (exercise, studying, walking your dog, socializing, warding off dust bunnies, etc.) at the top of the list. This will ensure that the most important things will always get done and also keep you in control of your life. And don't forget to include a little spare time or buffer zone to give yourself a breather—even organized people need a little "me" time.

## First things first: Wake up early!

They say the early bird gets the worm. Well, Mom says the early bird has a better day because it's more organized! Go ahead and make yourself set that alarm clock thirty minutes earlier than you had planned. It will give you time to wake up, get some caffeine, take a shower, read the paper, or catch the morning news, and assures that you will be early, or at least on time.

If you hit the snooze button more than once, more than likely you will be running late all day. That's no way to be organized! Make that decision to go ahead and get up, even if it's hard. Actually, do it especially if it's hard. If getting up in the morning is not your favorite thing to do, you probably aren't a morning person, and that's all the more reason to roll on out of bed a little bit earlier and give yourself time to wake up. Who knows who you may meet this morning, or what exciting opportunities await you? And you will miss it all if you're still pressing the snooze, or if you're groggy, rushed, and frazzled!

Have a nice day!

## Make a list.

Get in the habit of writing everything down. Make a list for everything. Writing down phone numbers, names, and notes will unclutter your mind and help you keep up with information. It also keeps you from forgetting things, like that pop quiz on Friday, that volunteer work you signed up for, or that sweet Mother's Day card you're planning to buy! (*Couldn't resist.*)

Keep a small notebook, note pad, or calendar in a central location where you can easily find it. If you do this, you can eliminate sticky notes, random (and easily lost) scraps of paper, and the chance that you might forget something important. If you are computer savvy, use software to create electronic reminders for your important categories. (Mom is not, and therefore I have no idea what I just said, but I'm sure this can be done.)

## Learn and use technology.

Okay, since I mentioned *technology* in the previous paragraph, I suppose I should elaborate. I do realize that you Facebooking, iPhoning kids know more about technology than many of us Moms ever will—we still think a BlackBerry is something you eat—but the truth remains that technology is a wonderful organizational tool. The little bit I have utilized has made my life easier. Technology can simplify your life if you understand how to make it work for you.

## Technology tips

* Sign up for on-line checking
* Sign up for automatic bill payments on-line
* Buy stamps on-line
* Program phone numbers and contact info into your cell phone

### Always be on time.

Doesn't it bug you when someone comes in late to a meeting or an appointment? Make a real effort not to be that person. It is rude and shows no respect for another person's time. Of course there are always instances when a late arrival cannot be prevented. If this does happen to you, make every effort to offer an honest and heartfelt apology. If time permits and you know you are going to be late, make a phone call and let the other person know. It is simply common courtesy.

### Establish routines to keep a tidy home, car, etc.

Routines can make the world a better place! You know I am right. Establishing routines will make sure you "stay on top" of your life. You take care of the little things so that everything doesn't pile up on you. You don't have to be overwhelmed; you can work *smarter* (by making and keeping routines), so you don't have to work *harder* by playing catch-up all the time. How? Keep a running balance in your checkbook, back up your computer once a week, make your bed every day, clean out the refrigerator before you go shopping, and clean the junk out of your car each time you get out of it. Spending a little time to stay organized makes your life more pleasant—and saves you time in the long run.

**MOM-*sense*:** Don't walk out of a room unless you leave it better than you found it. Get in the habit of carrying something with you as you go from room to room, and put things back in their place.

# Now, let's take a little walk for an area-by-area organizational tour of the house . . .

**Bedroom:** Okay, I know what you're going to say: "I don't have time to make my bed in the morning." Well, Mom just rolled her eyes at that one. Everyone has time to make his or her bed in the morning. It only takes about three minutes and makes a big difference! So, let go of that tired "I don't have time" excuse. Make the bed for a week and just see how good it feels to come home to a neat, inviting room.

And by the way, don't let your bed be the landing spot for every piece of clothing that you take off or for the ones that you tried on and decided not to wear. (Yes, Mom knows you do this.) Hang up your clean clothes, put the dirty ones in the laundry basket or hamper, and pick up the stuff all over the floor. Put all those shoes sitting everywhere away where they belong—or else you'll waste time hunting for them tomorrow. There! Now your room is all neat and tidy again.

Those seven minutes it took you to do that sure were exhausting, weren't they? Mom doesn't think so, and neither should you.

**MOM-*sense*:** On your way to bed, do a quick "nighttime walk through"; put things in their place and straighten up. The next morning it will be nice to wake up to a new day—and a neat place.

**Bathroom:** Bathrooms can be wonderful if they are clean, shiny, and smell good. Actually, there is not much that is nicer than a clean bathroom, and there is nothing worse than a dirty one. You know exactly what I mean. Keep your personal items put away in a medicine cabinet or in drawers. Make sure you have fresh soap for hand washing and a clean towel for drying. Keep the toilet tissue refilled, and the toilet bowl and seat clean. The shower or tub needs to

be cleaned once a week. It isn't too time-consuming if you just put little things away while you are brushing your teeth or washing your face. Don't neglect this room, or you may be embarrassed when a friend drops by and asks to use the restroom.

**Closets:** Keep your closets neat and orderly so that you can see what you have in there. It is also a great idea to rearrange your clothing when the seasons change. Bring the new season's clothes to the front of the line and move the others to the back. It will make such a difference when you are looking for that favorite sweater or pair of pants.

Shoes can be a whole other problem. They seem to multiply if left in a pile for too long. Solution? Don't leave them there. Buy an inexpensive shoe rack to get them off the floor, or a shoe bag for the back of a door. Don't keep shoes that you will never wear. Box them up and donate them to a charity that accepts clothing and shoes (only if they are in good shape—otherwise, to the garbage bin).

**MOM-*sense*:** Be sure to clean up your shoes if they are dirty. Nothing looks worse than a pair of dirty shoes, and Mom raised you better than that.

**Cabinets:** If your cabinets are not organized, be careful when you open those doors; something might fall on you. It doesn't take much time at all to straighten a cabinet. Take everything out and place it back in, with the tallest items in the back, and taper down as you come toward the front. Only stack items that stack well and don't teeter. Always turn labels toward the front. It is always nice to open a cabinet door and actually be able to find what you are looking for.

**Kitchen:** Please, please, please keep this room clean. (Do it for Mom's sake if not your own. Make a habit of putting food away. Let someone else support the ant and rodent population.) Also, be sure that foods are stored in the proper ways. Keep your sink empty by either loading the dishwasher each day or washing the dishes if you don't have a dishwasher. Keep cleaning products handy and use them often, especially antibacterial sprays, wipes, and soaps. Keep your floor free of crumbs.

This room should be the cleanest and most organized that you have. Check out the housekeeping chapter on page 35 to find great tips and ideas for cleaning your icky refrigerator and all those other spots in your kitchen. You can do it!

**Countertops:** Clutter on countertops can be so annoying. I know this Mom hates it. Whether it is the kitchen, bathroom, or another room in your place, clear it off. Everything you have should have a place where it belongs. Put things away and find a home for it if it doesn't have one already. Nothing looks worse than a countertop that has junk all over it. Oh, and when you clear it off, it might need a little wipe off with a cleaning product.

**MOM-*sense*:** If you already have a landslide of clutter everywhere, set your timer for ten minutes each day—then go on a clearing-and-throwing-away rampage! Before too many days, you will be able to see your counters and tabletops again.

**Living Areas:** Okay, picture this: A group of friends drops by on their way to a game, and they wind up standing around because your sofa and chair are covered with dirty clothes and newspapers. Don't let this happen to you, or more importantly, to them. Pick up your place and be proud of your home. Make it inviting, and keep it neat; no one wants to hang out in a pigsty. Stack the papers, magazines, and catalogs neatly. Pick up the glasses, cups, and cereal bowls and put them away. Fluff the pillows. Water that wilting plant. Gather all clothes that are vacationing on the couch and return them to their homes. Remember, just a few minutes here and there will keep your place presentable and help you feel good about your house. Then you can feel free to invite someone over and truly welcome drop-in guests, rather than having a nervous breakdown.

**Car:** Our cars are often an extension of our living spaces. Sometimes we spend so much time in them, they become a mobile living room. Because we do spend so much time in our cars, we tend to get a little too comfortable and bring more and more stuff into those small spaces. Not only do we fill our cars with junk, we also dine in them as well. Before long, they're a cross between a diner and a trashcan. Yuck!

Since there's so much going on in our autos, we'll need to practice our organizational skills here as well. It is a good idea to clean your vehicle each time you exit. This means taking out the coffee cups, soda cans, water bottles, gum wrappers, fast food bags, papers, and clothes. If you neglect keeping your car clean, it will become disgusting pretty fast (and may even end up smelling like a fast-food joint or locker room). Remember, it only takes a few minutes to do a little cleanup so that your next passenger won't be asking for a shovel and some air freshener.

There are a few essentials that everyone needs to keep in their car. (No, I'm not talking about Bose speakers and GPS systems.) Some things you will need every day; others, only every now and then. And, some you will never need

> ## THINGS TO KEEP IN THE CAR
>
> ✓ CD organizer that fits on sun visor (*so Mom doesn't worry that you're combing the floor for that new CD while driving*)
>
> ✓ Cell phone charger
>
> ✓ First aid kit
>
> ✓ Flashlight and extra batteries
>
> ✓ Hand/wet wipes
>
> ✓ Map
>
> ✓ Registration Information
>
> ✓ Sunglass clip for the visor
>
> ✓ Umbrella
>
> ✓ Proof-of-insurance card

(unless you get pulled over by the police), but you should have them on-hand anyway.

If you commute, or if you frequently visit family or some special someone on the weekends, you need to stock your auto with a few extra items. After all, you never know when an emergency will happen. Keep a small box, bag, or basket in your trunk or rear compartment to contain these items. You can buy these important essentials at a discount store or an auto parts dealer. Some places even sell an emergency kit that has all kinds of things inside.

Mom hopes that you will never need any of these. But it is better to be safe than sorry, so be prepared and drive safely. Oh, and call Mom to let her know you arrived without a hitch. She will be happy to hear your voice.

## EXTRA CAR ESSENTIALS FOR ROAD TRIPS OR DAILY COMMUTES

- ✓ Bottled water
- ✓ Flares
- ✓ Gloves
- ✓ Help sign (folded up)
- ✓ Jumper cables
- ✓ Swiss Army knife
- ✓ Tire inflator (like Fix-A-Flat)

## Tend to the mail.

When you pick up your mail, what do you do with it? Do you look through it and then plop it down on the counter? Well, if you do, then you are just like most people in the world: unorganized. It only takes a couple of minutes of your time to keep that mail from piling up, and those bills (yes, you'll have them) from getting lost.

**MOM-*sense*:** Grab a highlighter and mark names and numbers that you look up in the phone book. The next time you need that number, it will be easier for you to find.

## Tips for Handling the Mail

- ★ Open all the mail.
- ★ Toss out the junk.
- ★ File things that don't need immediate attention. *(You will need to have a box or folder already prepared with a system in mind.)*
- ★ Keep bills that need to be paid in a central location.
- ★ Respond to invitations ASAP, without any delay.
- ★ Put magazines and catalogs in a neat stack. (And perhaps throw away the old ones to make room for the replacements!)
- ★ Enjoy the clutter-free counter.

## Deal with paper. *(It won't magically disappear.)*

If you have sorted the mail, then everything is now in its place, right? Well, sort of . . . Okay, Moms know that sometimes we all get a little behind or distracted. So you didn't do such a good job with the mail and you left out some papers from a project you're working on, and now you have a mess on your hands?

Ah, paper, paper, paper, what to do with all that paper! Even in this technology-advanced world, paper is a big part of our daily lives. It piles up at work, school, and home. Sometimes all that paper makes you want to pull your hair out. Instead, just take a minute and relax. Mom has a foolproof solution. Ready? First you need to make a plan for where each type of paper should go, and then—this is the hard part—*make sure you put it there.* (Even perfect plans are useless if you don't execute them.) Just get on it.

When dealing with paperwork of any kind, you always need to decide what to keep and what to discard. If you have neglected things and you have piles, begin by sorting everything into smaller piles. First deal with the urgent, pending, and very important issues: Start by paying the bills. (It's no fun to overlook a bill and find yourself brushing your teeth in the dark with no electricity, facing credit issues.)

If you choose to pay your bills the old-fashioned way, by writing checks, you will need a few supplies. Envelopes, stamps, return address labels, a calculator, pen, pencil, and staples will make this job easier. Keep all these supplies in one convenient location and choose a time each month to sit down, pay your bills, and put them in the mail.

After you have paid the bills, attack the rest of the paper stash. Inevitably there will be many papers you will need to keep, so it is a good idea to begin a filing system. No, you don't need to go out and buy a bulky four-drawer filing cabinet. You can use a box or drawer and accomplish the same thing. You will need to buy some folders and label them. File them alphabetically, and you should have an easy time with this task. You might even want to keep a file at the front for bills whose due dates are a few weeks off so you don't forget about them.

## TIPS FOR AN ORDERLY FILING SYSTEM—INCLUDE THESE CATEGORIES WHEN LABELING YOUR FILES

- One file for the bills you pay (or you could have a file for each one individually) kept in A-B-C order
- **Appliance Manuals** – oven, dishwasher, refrigerator, washer & dryer, etc.
- **Auto** – receipts for repairs
- **Bank** – include statements and deposit receipts
- **Donations** – receipts for charitable donations
- **Home** – receipts for purchases like furniture, jewelry, and home improvements
- **Insurance** – auto, home, renters, medical, and life
- **Medical** – all medical and dental records
- **Pet** – veterinary records
- **Tax** – receipts for completing your tax returns

**For items that need more security than a cardboard file box:**

As you accumulate items and need a more secure place to keep important papers, consider renting a safety deposit box at your local bank. These are minimally priced and offer peace of mind. Items you might want to keep in a safety deposit box are things that would be hard or nearly impossible to replace. A safety deposit box is easily obtained and can be accessed at any time during banking hours. It is a good idea to not rent a safety deposit box in your name only. Add a parent or sibling to the rental agreement. Not only is it smart to have someone else know where your important things are, but in case of death, these boxes are usually sealed. Always inform at least one other person where your important things are located.

## ITEMS COMMONLY KEPT IN A SAFE DEPOSIT BOX

* Adoption or Citizenship Papers
* Auto Titles and Property Deeds
* Birth and/or Death Certificates
* Bond and Stock Certificates
* Expensive Jewelry Receipts and Appraisals
* Passports
* Savings Bonds
* Trust Papers, Wills, Power of Attorney Documents

## Keep current with cameras, film, and photographs.

I'll just bet that you have an old roll of film in the back of a drawer that needs to be developed. (Well, maybe not. I keep forgetting that we are living in the age of digital cameras.) Okay, how about a disc full of photos that got stuck somewhere because: A) you were too lazy to download it or get the photos developed, or B) you bought a new disc because you misplaced the full one? Whatever the answer, try to get in the habit of taking care of your photos very soon after you have snapped them.

Speaking of photographs, see the box for my instructions on hanging a picture or painting on your wall.

## HANG A PICTURE ON THE WALL IN SIX EASY STEPS

**1**. Have your items ready: picture, hammer, picture hanger and nail, tape measure, and pencil.

**2**. Hold your picture in the spot where you want it and gently make a mark on the wall at the top of the frame with the pencil.

**3**. Using your tape measure, measure between the wire holder on the back of the picture and the top of the frame. *Hint: pull the wire tight toward the top with the tape measure for accuracy.*

**4**. Using that measurement, take your tape measure and measure from the original mark on the wall and make a new one below it with the photo/wire measurement.

**5**. Place your picture hanger's bottom on the new mark and hammer it into place.

**6**. Hang your picture and admire your skills.

**Note:** If your picture doesn't have a wire across the back, but does have the little jagged zig-zagged piece of hardware, use the same approach, just measure to the center of the hardware piece. You may only need a nail.

### PHOTO REMINDERS

◆ Download photos shortly after taking them.

◆ Print photos from your downloads, or take the disc to a developer.

◆ Put photos into albums or store in photo boxes.

◆ Try to store photos in a dated order.

◆ Share photos with friends and family.

◆ Enjoy looking at your photos.

## Recycle!

Make Mom proud; do your part to save the planet. If you aren't that gung-ho about recycling, you can feel good about getting rid of more waste. By creating new products from old ones, recycling actually keeps useful things from becoming waste in the first place.

If everyone recycled their household recyclables, our landfills would have much less in them. Come on, it isn't as hard as you think. Many things that you use in your everyday life can be recycled. Think about all the things you toss

- Aluminum cans
- Cardboard
- Glass
- Newspapers
- Plastic bottles
- Plastic grocery store bags
- Tin food cans

*Note: This list only covers household-type items; you can recycle many other products as well.*

in the garbage. If you recycle, you can reduce your amount of garbage substantially. Keep a box or shopping bags handy to place recyclables in. Some communities and cities have curbside pick-up, but in other areas, you will need to take your items to a facility for drop off. They will need to be separated into their respective types before depositing.

While we're on the subject, try using some reusable bags for your shopping. Canvas bags work great, plus many grocery and discount stores sell reusable bags for a minimal price (as low as 99 cents) to help you control waste. These bags typically hold more than the plastic kind and you won't be throwing anything away when your groceries are put in their place. Just keep them in your car and use them every time you shop. You'll be doing one more thing to help save our planet.

## Make some plans.

Doesn't it just drive you crazy when someone waits until the last minute to invite you to do something? (My husband says I used to be one of these people.) It is a really bad habit and not very thoughtful. It simply makes more sense to plan ahead and eliminate the chance that you will be stuck all alone with your TV for the night. Now, of course, there will always be spontaneous parties, eating out, and movie nights. But for the most part, try to be considerate and plan ahead.

Get in the habit of thinking forward. Be on the lookout for unique restaurants, watch for new movies, and read the newspaper to check for sporting events, concerts, plays, and whatever else is out there. Be informed and equipped to invite someone to attend an event with you, and before long, people may be calling you to see "what's going on."

I've tried to be thorough, but even I'm not perfect. So, here are some answers to a few questions you may still have . . .

## What if I don't have room for a filing cabinet?
No problem. Buy a banker's box or a file box at your local discount or office supply store. They are inexpensive ways to hold hanging files, and you can slide them under a bed or place them in a closet.

## How long should I keep my daily receipts?
Hang on to those credit card, ATM, and debit receipts until you post them and check them against their statements. Then shred away.

## What do I need for the IRS?
The Internal Revenue Service recommends that an individual keep records for at least three years. This includes bank statements with copies of cancelled checks, income tax returns, and any pertinent receipts for large purchases or payments. After three to six months, get rid of receipts that you do not need for tax purposes; they only take up space. Only keep them for reference, customer service numbers, and documentation that you paid your bills. Look at www.irs.gov for more information.

# Just one more thing . . .
(Okay, it's more than one, but you're used to that by now, aren't you?)

☞ **Fill 'er up.** Don't let your gas tank get below ¼ full. It can go fast once you pass that point, and I guarantee it is never a convenient time to fill up an almost empty tank.

☞ **Keep a list of customer service phone numbers for all cards you carry in your wallet.**

**Call immediately if lost or stolen!**
*This includes*:

- ATM and bank cards
- Credit cards
- Driver's license
- Library card
- Social Security card
- Voter registration card
- Work I.D.

☞ **Got 5 or 10 minutes to kill?**
- Call someone you need to check on (perhaps an old friend, a relative, *your Mom??*).
- Clean out your wallet or purse.
- Do a quick checkbook balance.
- Sort through your stack of magazines—or take a minute to read one.
- Make a list for shopping.
- Plan some meals.
- Sew on that button that fell off.
- Toss in a load of laundry.
- Unload the dishwasher.
- Write someone a note of thanks or friendship.

☞ **Don't be a quitter.** Complete and finish what you are doing before you start a new project.

# CHAPTER TWO

# Loads about Laundry

*"Everybody has their own dirty laundry."*

Of course, that line has a deeper meaning, but the basic fact remains true: we all have to wash our underwear. Some of you have been sorting and sudsing for years, but for others, the world of detergents, fabric softeners, and spin cycles is strange new territory. So we're going to go over the basics of how to actually "do the laundry."

Whether you have a home washing machine and dryer, or you do your laundry somewhere else, a few do's and don'ts can make the job go more smoothly. By following Mom's suggestions, you won't just look great; you may also end up being the one your friends call when they want to know how to get ketchup off their sweater.

## First things first: Know your laundry basics.

Always remember this basic truth: *Laundry has a tendency to grow if left alone for too long.* The basket begins to overflow, the piles reach toward the sky, and despite your good wishes, the stains and smells won't disappear all by themselves. So enough talking about it, just get to it. Let's get started . . .

### Laundry Rule #1: Purchase your laundry-cleaning supplies before you start.

If you are confused when you face those shelves full of cleaners and softeners, call your Mom and ask what she uses. Chances are you like the way your laundry smells when your Mom does it. See a sample laundry list on the next page.

### Laundry Rule #2: Sorting or separating your clothing is a definite must before you take another step.

If you are not fortunate enough to have learned laundry basics at home, pay attention. Begin by separating your clothing by color. Whites, darks, and lights are the typical divisions. Whites and lights can be done together if you are short on time, money, or washing machine space, but NEVER wash dark clothes with light or white clothes.

Don't believe Mom? Just try it and see how your favorite white shirt looks after being washed with a red sock or washcloth. (It's amazing how quickly white becomes pink.) As for textures and different types of fabrics, use common sense. Wash items like towels with other towels. Don't stick a white fluffy towel in the same load as your new blouse or corduroy pants, or you will have lint all over them.

Finally, sort your clothing according to how dirty they are. Clothes that are excessively soiled should not be washed with other items that are not as dirty. The less-dirty clothing may not come out as clean. It is a good idea to soak very dirty clothing in soapy water and rinse before washing them with a load of laundry.

> **MOM-*sense*:** Turn corduroys wrong-side out when laundering. The "pile" of the fabric will stand up better and look much nicer if you wash and dry them this way.

### Laundry Rule #3: Always read the labels in your clothes.

Don't wash anything whose label reads "dry-clean only," and don't spend money on dry-cleaning when you can wash an article of clothing yourself. Some items may instruct you to "lie flat" or "hang dry," while others may say "tumble dry low" to limit the dryer's heat impact. (Dryers on too hot of a cycle can shrink clothing.)

## LAUNDRY SHOPPING LIST

**Laundry basket or bag:** Not an expensive item, but be sure it is big enough to hold a week's worth of dirty clothes.

**Detergent:** So many choices you'll want to scream! Powders, liquids, or concentrates are your first decision. Choose yours and follow the directions on the label. Understand that the new concentrated liquids mean that you won't need to add as much to your load of laundry. And if you do choose a powder, you may want to add it while the water is pouring in and then swish it around until it dissolves.

**Bleach:** Liquid or powder? The general rule of thumb is to use liquid chlorine bleach for white clothing and powdered bleach for colors. You  will not need to use bleach in every white load, only those that are especially faded or stained. And use bleach with caution! My husband still laments the time I ruined his favorite blue shirt shortly after we married.

**Fabric softeners/Dryer sheets:** Fabric softeners are used in the washing machine and are typically added to the rinse water. Dryer sheets are a little easier to use, tossed into the dryer with each load of clothing. Either choice will help your clothes to smell fresh and not have the dreaded static cling.

**Stain remover:** Do not forget this one. Choices will include sprays or sticks to rub on the stain. Also, the new stain stick pens and wipes are handy items to keep on you in case of accidents. If you use one of these little jewels soon after your spill, smudge, or smear, your stains will come clean better.

Clothing that looks like it should be dry-cleaned may just be delicate. If so, wash your delicates together on the delicate cycle of the washing machine. These cycles usually run a shorter time span.

**MOM-*sense*:** Ladies, to protect delicate lingerie items or hosiery, purchase a zippered lingerie bag to keep them safe during the washing process, or wash on the delicate cycle.

### Laundry Rule #4: Pretreat those stains and spots.

Check your clothes before you load them into the machine. Spray or rub a stain remover on the item before you wash. If you fail to do this and go ahead with the washing and drying process, the stain can "set," as my Mom used to say, and become difficult to remove later. Try checking the pretreated clothing after washing and before drying. If the spot didn't completely disappear, try the process one more time.

One typical area to find stains is on the front of shirts. Mom knows this because I just may hold the world record for spilling things down the front of mine. Please check your shirt-fronts so that you won't look like me. Also, check the collars of shirts, sleeve cuffs, and the seats of your pants.

### Laundry Rule #5: Empty those pockets!

Whatever you do, take the time to empty the pockets of pants, shorts, skirts, jackets, and shirts. You may find something you had thought was lost, and you just might prevent damage to your clothes or the washing machine (you'd never guess how much havoc a little ballpoint pen can wreak). I have personally accumulated quite a nice little sum of money over the years from emptying pockets.

### Laundry Rule #6: Zip up those zippers, turn everything right-side out, and fasten those hooks.

Also, turn down those rolled up shirtsleeves. Your clothes will come out cleaner if you simply take the time to make sure they are at their maximum potential for becoming clean. This is also a good time to check for missing buttons, torn hems, and other damages.

### CHOOSE THE CORRECT WATER TEMPERATURE.

Most washing machines have at least three settings for water temperature: Cold, Hot, and Warm. Moms know that choosing the wrong water temperature can cause you lots of problems. Clothes can shrink, colors can fade and bleed onto other clothing, and whites can become gray.

## COMMON STAINS AND REMOVAL TECHNIQUES

**Blood**: Mix equal parts of ammonia and water together and soak the item. Don't use bleach because it will not work on bloodstains. You can also try your own saliva. Yes, it's odd, but I've heard from reliable sources that it works.

**Chewing gum**: Freeze the entire item by placing it in your freezer or use an ice cube on a small area. You should be able to scrape off the hardened gum with a dull knife.

**Chocolate**: Soak the item in cold water for fifteen minutes and then rinse it under cold running water.

**Coffee/Tea**: Rub the item with a mixture that is one part vinegar and three parts water.

**Deodorant**: Sponge the stain with white vinegar and then rinse with cold water.

**Ink**: Spray thoroughly with an inexpensive aerosol hairspray. Rinse with cold water. If stain remains, try a mixture of ½ cup of alcohol and 1 cup water. Rub into the stain until it is gone. Rinse and launder.

**Lipstick**: Rub with petroleum jelly and then launder as usual.

**Makeup**: Pretreat with your stain remover and then launder.

**Mustard**: Rinse with cold water and rub in a small amount of liquid detergent. Let this set overnight, apply some stain remover, and launder.

**Red Wine**: If you have white wine, pour some on the red stain. Quickly shake some salt onto the area and then wash.

**White Wine**: Use cold water with two shakes of salt and a little lemon juice.

**HOT WATER** is recommended for white clothes and clothes that are heavily soiled. The temperature is usually around 130 degrees F.

**WARM WATER** is probably what you'll use the most. The temperature is about 90 degrees F. Warm water washes are for light-colored clothing, lightly soiled, and permanent press type items.

**COLD WATER** is roughly 80 degrees F. Cold-water washes are for bright-and dark-colored clothing. This setting is also good for delicate items or clothing at risk to fade or shrink.

Now that you have chosen your cleaners, sorted your clothes, and selected a temperature setting, load those clothes and let the machine do its work. As soon as a cycle is complete, remove your clothing and begin the drying process.

**MOM-*sense*:** Add one cup of white vinegar to your rinse cycle instead of your fabric softener. The vinegar will soften your clothes because it cuts through the residue that the detergent can leave on your clothing. This is wonderful for anyone who has sensitive skin.

## DRY THOSE CLEAN CLOTHES *TODAY.*

First things first . . . empty the lint trap. This can prevent fires and will also assure that the dryer works more efficiently. The lint trap is a screen that usually slides into a slot on the front of the dryer just inside the door. Simply wipe it off and toss the lint into the garbage. *Do this every single time you use the dryer.*

Next to leaving the lint trap so full that it looks like gray cotton candy, Mom's other drying pet peeve is leaving freshly cleaned clothes in the washer too long.  I'm sure you've never thought of doing this, but I've heard of people neglecting their clean, *wet* laundry for so many days that when they finally open the washer door to throw them in the dryer, they are greeted with the lovely smell of mildew. Yuck! You don't want to have to run a load of towels or clothes twice, do you? Or possibly have to throw them out? Get in the habit of moving clothes straight to the dryer as soon as the washing cycle ends.

**Temperature settings:** Most of your wash can be dried on a medium temperature setting. Typically you will only need the high heat settings for towels. Low temperatures are better for delicate items that you do not want to shrink.

**Shake out your clothes:** Do this as you switch them from the washing machine to the dryer. It will take longer to dry your clothes if you toss them into the dryer in a large heaping pile. Also, there will be fewer wrinkles if you take the time to shake each item and toss it in.

**Don't over-dry:** It is not a good idea to over-dry your clothing. This can cause your clothes to have too many wrinkles or even shrink. Check your load as it runs through its cycle to gauge how quickly your clothes are drying.

> **MOM-*sense*:** To eliminate wrinkles and shrinkage, you will want to take some items out and hang them up before they dry completely. If you do it just right, you may not have to iron much at all!

**Unload the dryer:** Take your clothes out and fold them while they are still warm. Allowing them to sit in the dryer will guarantee you clean clothes full of wrinkles. Just take a few minutes to do this minor task. And thank Mom when you've got ten minutes to get dressed and don't have to get out the ironing board.

**Put your laundry away:** While you've got some Momentum, go ahead and put that clean, folded laundry away. It will help you avoid clothes pile-ups, and there is nothing

nicer than clean, folded laundry that is put back in its own space.

There, now you understand the basics of laundry. But just in case you think you forgot a detail or two, here's a quick reminder list:

## A LAUNDRY LIST OF REMINDERS

❖ Buy your laundry detergent and supplies.
❖ Sort your clothing.
❖ Treat your stains.
❖ Check for damages or missing buttons.
❖ Wash.
❖ Dry.
❖ Hang and/or fold.
❖ Iron (see next section).
❖ Put clean laundry away.

> **MOM-*sense*:** Try to get on a "laundry schedule," especially for sheets and towels. A schedule helps you avoid a laundry pile-up.

# Iron away those pesky wrinkles.

And now to one of my favorite topics: ironing! Yes, I am an ironing fanatic—my family thinks it is a disease. The truth is, I simply despise wrinkled clothes. And based on years of steaming and pressing, here is my ironing advice.

**Ironing supplies needed:** You will need an iron, an ironing board, and a spray bottle for water, starch, or sizing. For irons, you can choose between steam or dry. Most irons you can purchase today come equipped with an automatic safety shut-off feature. These are clever safety gadgets, great in case you forget to turn the iron off or it falls over. The ironing board should have a tight-fitting cover so that your job of ironing will be smooth. Starch and sizing can be found with the laundry products where you shop. Starches can make your clothing crisp, while sizing can help eliminate wrinkles and give body back to your clothes. They are not necessary, but can help—and they're a must if you want to join the professional/ fanatic/"diseased" ranks like Mom.

## KNOW WHICH CLOTHES YOU WILL DRY-CLEAN, AND WHERE.

To dry-clean or not to dry-clean, that is the question! Well, that probably isn't the question, but it can often be a dilemma. And even though dry-cleaning can be expensive, it is wise to dry-clean your finer pieces of clothing like suits, dresses, silks, and nicer sweaters made of wool, as well as items you do not trust yourself to wash at the local Laundromat.

Before you decide to dry-clean, read your labels and look at the fabrics. *Hand washing* is an option for some items that are simply delicate and need a little extra time and care. Some liquid detergents,

## IRONING DO'S & DON'TS

☞ **Do** read the labels in your clothes for the proper temperature setting.

☞ **Don't** begin with the temperature on the highest setting and scorch your clothing.

☞ **Do** take damp clothing straight from the dryer if you want it ironed.

☞ **Don't** push down with your iron— smooth back and forth strokes are better.

☞ **Do** mist-spray dry clothes with water for a better ironing job.

☞ **Don't** spray water on silk, or you will leave water spots.

☞ **Do** iron collars, hems, sleeves, and cuffs first.

☞ **Don't** put on a pair of pants you've just ironed until they cool—ouch!

☞ **Do** iron silks, rayon, and wool clothing on the wrong side at low settings.

☞ **Do** watch a favorite movie or TV show while ironing if you have a lot to iron! (Mom's ironed many a shirt to *American Idol*.)

like Woolite, are especially made for hand washing. Remember it is your choice (and your money).

If you do take the dry-cleaning route, be sure and remove the plastic bags from your dry-cleaned clothing right when you bring them home. This helps them air out so you will not inhale the laundering chemicals when you open the bags. Also, if you notice a very strong chemical smell, your clothing is probably not dry or has too much dry-cleaning solvent in it. Air these out for a day, and if the smell doesn't leave, use a new dry-cleaner next time around.

**MOM-*sense*:** To find a good dry-cleaner, ask friends or co-workers who have lived in the area a while. A good dry-cleaner will have a reputation that will set him or her apart. Mom has used the same dry-cleaner for over twenty years, and we even exchange Christmas cards. It is worth taking the time to ask around.

## MASTER MINOR REPAIRS.

We've all lost a button or pulled a hem out of a pair of pants. But don't fret: you, too, can fix these minor mishaps and not miss a beat. Chances are you don't have a seamstress as a best friend, so learn some minor mending yourself. Buying a sewing kit is a good place to start. You can purchase a small one at any grocery store or convenience market. Mom likes

to collect the tiny ones that hotels place on their bathroom counters. If you spend a little time doing repairs when they happen, you won't be so disappointed the next time you put on your favorite shirt and find the middle button is missing.

### Sewing List

★**Thread**: White, black, navy, brown, and gray should be enough.

★**Needles**: An assorted package will do.

★**Straight pins**: You need just a few in a pincushion or small box.

★**Safety pins**: These are for emergency situations, to hold things together.

★**Scissors**: You'll find they work better than your teeth.

★**Buttons**: A package of odd buttons can be found at any discount store.

**Minor clothing repairs:** Just think how competent you'll feel once you master these small tasks. And Mom will be so proud!

## 1. Sew on a button.

Thread a needle, double the thread, and knot the end twice. Start with the needle under the fabric and push it up through the fabric and one of the buttonholes. Pull the thread tight. Push the needle back down through the other hole and the fabric. Repeat these steps until you feel the button is secure. Finish with the needle and thread on the underside of the fabric, cut the thread and tie off into a knot.

## 2. Fix a fallen hem.

**The easy method**: Use iron-fusible tape that you can buy with sewing supplies. Place the tape between the hem and the garment and simply iron it into place. The tape will fuse the hem back together. This is a glorious product that you will love.

**The durable method**: Pin the hem in place with straight pins. With a needle threaded with doubled thread, make small stitches around the fallen hem. Don't pull the thread too tightly. At the end, knot the thread securely. When finished, iron the clothing using steam.

**MOM-*sense*:** In an emergency situation, you can use tape or, if you must, a stapler to fix a hem that has fallen out. Remember this fix is only temporary, and you should repair it with a needle and thread as soon as possible.

## 3. Repair a split seam.

Turn the clothing inside out. Using a needle with doubled thread, and with the seam edges pinned together, make small stitches and overlap them for extra strength.

## 4. Hire someone to do more complicated repairs.

You will need to find a seamstress or tailor shop to make more extensive repairs that you may not be ready to attempt. Some examples of these include

* **Lengthening or shortening hems**

* **Replacing broken zippers**

* **Replacing broken elastic**

* **Altering clothing that has become too small or too large**

* **Repairing or replacing the lining of coats or pants**

Many dry-cleaners will have a seamstress on staff, just ask. Although some repairs can be a tad pricey, good and affordable shops are out there; you just need to do a little research.

## Do I always have to wash everything I wear even if it still seems clean?

Not necessarily. Often you can get by with wearing things more than once. Hang up your jeans, jackets, sweaters, and suits immediately after wearing. Dry-cleaned items can usually be worn more than once, too. (But if you see a big ink stain, ketchup blob, or your clothing smells like a Mexican restaurant, throw it in the washer, babe.)

## If I'm in a bind, can I use some other type of soap besides laundry detergent in the washing machine?

No way, no how. Dishwashing liquid, shampoo, or other cleaners can lead to an abundance of bubbles that you will not want to clean up. It may look like fun on TV, but remember, those actors are making big bucks to clean up islands of bubbles; you're not.

## What can I do if my pillow smells funny?

If your pillow is a bit smelly and you don't want to buy a new one, toss it in the washing machine on a gentle cycle using cold water, and rinse and spin two times. Fluff it in the dryer for a few minutes on a low cycle, and then let it continue drying outside in the sun on a chair.

## Should I use fabric softener on my towels?

Not every time you wash them. Once a month is enough, because using fabric softener too often will make your towels less absorbent. And nobody likes a wimpy towel.

## What should I do if I spill something on my shirt in a restaurant?

Quickly get some club soda and a cloth napkin. Dip the napkin in the club soda, and rub the stain. It should help tremendously!

# Just one more thing . . .

✛**Don't overload the washing machine**. Your clothing will come out much cleaner if it has room to move around. Load it loosely and only fill it about ¾ full. (If you do overload it, you will be able to tell by the horrendous sound when the spin cycle begins. Your machine may even dance around the floor.)

✛**Always wash new linens before you put them on your bed**. Washing them will soften them, and they will smell better, too.

✛**Hang up those bath towels and use them again**. A wet bath towel thrown in a heap on the floor can be a starting place for mildew to grow. Your Mom didn't raise a slob.

✛**Designate a lost & found place for laundry**. Keep a basket handy for stray socks, buttons that have lost their home, and other odds and ends that only come out when the laundry is being done. Someday these items may find their way back home.

# CHAPTER THREE

# Handling Housekeeping

*"If you don't keep your house, it will keep you."*

You've heard of making mountains out of molehills? Without an intentional approach to housekeeping, pretty soon the molehills in your house (of clutter, clothes, dust, and grime) will turn into mountains! Avoiding ever having to face these mountains is part of what housekeeping is about.

You may have kept a messy room growing up. Well, you can shut the door on a messy room. You can hide things under the bed. But unless you plan on being a hermit, you can't shut the door on a messy house. And you can't throw everything under the couch, either.

But the good news is, Mom knows you are up to this task. When you follow the tips in this chapter, you can "keep up" with your house.

You can even make it sparkle and shine.

## First things first:
## Make time to clean.

Who has time to clean? Everyone says they don't, but the cleaning still needs to be done. The good news is that it doesn't have to be an all-day job. If you just get yourself on a routine, things won't be so bad. You probably lead a busy and hectic life. Surprise, we all do. No one wants to spend a day off from work or school, especially when it is gorgeous outside, cleaning the bathroom.

Housekeeping can be great therapy for you. Cleaning helps us to achieve some order in our lives and provides instant gratification. You will be proud of your place and how great it looks after you have cleaned it. There are many things in your life that you have no control over, like Mother Nature or who moves in next door, but you can keep your place clean.

**Accept the reality that you will need to clean your house regularly.**
I know: reality bites. Of course, you could live like a slob, but trust Mom, you won't have many friends who will want to visit often. You should want to live in a clean environment. Who wants a sink full of dirty dishes, dust on your coffee table so thick you can write your name in it, or a bathroom that is too scary to use. Besides, clean homes are healthier for you than dirty ones. Cleaning will help kill germs, reduce dust, and

disinfect your favorite areas to use. Read on for some more benefits of cleaning . . .

# Mom's Top Five Reasons for Cleaning Your House

### 1. Cleaning helps keep you healthy.

Like it or not, dust in your home can carry many particles that are unhealthy, and mold can make you sick as well. And think about all the dirt and who-knows-what that enters your house through your shoes. Germs are everywhere. Viruses and bacteria come from germs. You must destroy them.

### 2. Cleaning is a sort of investment in your home and your things.

Think about it: Wood furniture will fare better if dusted regularly. Rugs and carpets will last much longer if you vacuum them often. Electronics will function better and longer when regularly dusted. So, all those Moms in the fifties weren't just cleaning because they liked it; they were exhibiting good business sense!

### 3. Cleaning helps eliminate insects and rodents.

This one isn't rocket science either: Ants won't hang out in your kitchen if your counters are clean and food is stored in airtight containers. And mice and roaches don't linger in places where there are no crumbs or food for them.

## 4. Cleaning allows you to have friends over without being embarrassed.

You may get used to living among dust bunnies and dirty toilets, but just wait until the doorbell rings. You want to be proud of your place, not ashamed.

## 5. Cleaning helps keeps you and your home organized.

In the process of cleaning, you will put things away and will even find things that you thought were lost. Because your home is clean, you will be more organized and be able to accomplish so much more.

So you see, there are many reasons for you to get busy cleaning. You don't have to be a clean freak to make sure things are done right. Just take the time to do some cleaning. It's not that hard (and it will smell so much better)! Trust Mom—you'll be glad you did.

## Gather your cleaning supplies.

You will need to buy some cleaning supplies, and let me tell you, the choices out there can be mind-boggling. Cleaning supplies have pretty much gone high-tech since Mom was young. Today you can buy "disposable" everything. While all these new supplies may be handy and time-saving, they can also be more expensive. Keep this in mind when you are shopping.

You can still find the good old supplies from way back when, too. You know, the kind you mix with water and clean everything from grime off the kitchen sink to the tar off your car's floormats. And the newer all-purpose cleaners actually clean well and smell good. It is just a cleaning-supply buffet out there!

### CLEANING SUPPLY CHECKLIST:

✓ Plastic bucket or caddy to carry supplies from room to room
✓ Small broom and dustpan
✓ Rubber gloves
✓ Bathroom cleaner (can be a powder or spray)
✓ Mildew remover (usually a spray)
✓ Glass cleaner
✓ Toilet bowl cleaner
✓ Toilet scrub brush
✓ Toothbrush
✓ Furniture polish
✓ Kitchen/all-purpose cleaning spray
✓ Paper towels
✓ Cleaning cloths and rags
✓ Vacuum cleaner

## Consider cleaning "green."

Unfortunately, some cleaning products that have been on the market for years have been discovered to be more than a little tough on our environment. That's why, along with many other products, cleaning supplies have gone green, too. Many cleaners are now substituting natural ingredients for the harsher ones and putting products on the market that are more eco-friendly.

You will be able to find several of these products in grocery or discount stores. Others, you will need to order from catalogs or off the Internet. Eco-friendly products can cost a little more than national brand-type cleaning supplies, but if you order in bulk or larger quantities, you can get a price break.

**A Few Green/Eco-Friendly Cleaning Supply Brands:**
- Method
- Meyers
- Seventh Generation
- Shaklee

Many brands will claim to be safer, better, or greener than the next brand. It is basically a matter of choice. Some have great scents, and some are scent-free. If you choose to go the green route, do a little research and try out different products.

**Utilize homemade cleaners.**
Your grandmothers and great-grandmothers didn't have all the latest in cleaning supplies, but their homes were clean and smelled good. They knew how to use what they had on hand, and so can you. If you are on a budget and can't afford the latest in fancy cleaning products, then this is the route for you to

travel. You can do just as good a job with homemade cleaners and save money, too! Following are some of Mom's favorites.

### VINEGAR: WHO KNEW SUCH A SMELLY SUBSTANCE COULD CLEAN?!

Plain white vinegar is a wonderful cleaning tool. You can use vinegar to clean just about everything in your home. It is mild and can dissolve dirt and soap scum. Vinegar is even gentle enough to clean hardwood floors. It is a great deodorizer because it absorbs odors. (Don't worry, the vinegar smell goes away when it dries up!)

**Vinegar cleaning mixture:**
**1 c. white vinegar, 1 c. water**

*Mix, use, and store in a spray bottle.* *This mixture is great for kitchens and bathrooms, and floors, too.

**MOM-*sense*:** To clean toilets, pour undiluted white vinegar straight from the bottle directly into the toilet bowl and use your toilet brush to scrub away the dirty, yucky stuff.

# BAKING SODA: SO MANY USES, SUCH A SMALL BOX!

If you have never been introduced to the wonders of baking soda, you are in for a treat. Not merely for biscuits and baking, it is truly multi-talented. Read on for a list of some of the ways Mom loves to use it.

***Got smelly trash?***
Sprinkle baking soda in the bottom of your garbage can before inserting the bag to absorb those nasty odors.

***Out of toothpaste?***
Brush your teeth with soda. Put some on your toothbrush, dampen with water, and brush away.

***Upset tummy?***
Use one glass of water and 1 tsp. soda for a homemade antacid.

***Got a small grease fire on your stove?***
Don't use water—toss on the baking soda.

***Your toenails and fingernails look a little yellow?***
Make a paste of water and baking soda and scrub them well.

***Want a fresh-smelling refrigerator?***
Stick an open box in the back.

***Stinky shoes?***
Sprinkle just a little soda inside them.

***White clothes looking a little on the dingy side?***
Pour a little in the next load of wash you do.

***Can't see through your oven door?***
Rub some baking soda on the baked-on stains. Use a wet cloth on the soda and rinse it off with clean water.

***Got a rash or sunburn?***
Dump about ½ of a box into a lukewarm bath for soothing results.

What'd I tell you? Baking soda is a miracle-in-a-box!

## GET ON A CLEANING ROUTINE.

Establishing and maintaining a cleaning routine will assure you of a clean place to live in, and you'll feel great about having accomplished something. It is also much easier to maintain a clean place if you do it regularly. If you don't clean regularly and you just let things pile up, you'll be spending a lot more time cleaning when you do decide to get on it. Like I said before, clean smarter, not harder.

On the day you establish as "clean-up" day, the best plan is simply to go from room to room cleaning most everything you see. If you tackle your entire place on one specific day, you won't have to remember what you cleaned and what still needs to be cleaned. Just go for it. Now, even Mom doesn't hit *every* little corner on cleaning day, but do the best you can.

A general rule for cleaning is to *pick up before you clean up.* Yes, that means for you to do a walk-through and pick up all the things laying around on floors and chairs and countertops so that you can do a thorough job cleaning. (Of course, if you've been picking up every day along the way, this part won't take you long.) Trust Mom, your cleaning time will go faster if you have already tidied up before you start to actually clean.

Try doing a quick, thorough once-a-week cleaning for a month and see if it doesn't make your life a little less chaotic. Less chaos is always a good thing!

## CLEANING ROUTINE CHECKLIST:

✘Gather your cleaning supplies.
✘Turn on some upbeat music to set the tempo for your cleaning.
✘Change the linens on your bed and make up the bed.
✘Gather dirty laundry together and wash it, or at least put it near the washing machine.
✘Clean the kitchen countertops and sink.
✘Wipe off all small appliances.
✘Wash dishes or load the dishwasher, run it, then put the clean dishes away.
✘Sweep and clean the kitchen floor.
✘Vacuum all carpeted areas and rugs.
✘Dust and polish the wood furniture in all rooms.
✘Wipe all knick-knacks clean of dust.
✘Clean glass doors and wipe fronts of TVs.
✘Dust the tops of frames hanging on the walls.
✘Wipe bathroom counters clean.
✘Clean the toilet, bathroom floor, and shower or tub.
✘Sit down and relax with a good book, or watch a movie, enjoying your clean surroundings.

**Be sure to keep a clean kitchen.**
Ah the kitchen . . . the heart of the home. Though the kitchen should be the cleanest room in everyone's home, it's often the dirtiest. Kitchens are typically the places where we all congregate or just stand around and talk while we nibble or graze. With all the coming, going, and standing it endures, it can be a real challenge to keep clean. Kitchen floors catch all the crumbs we drop, and the sink and countertops are excellent places for bacteria to grow.

Grossed out yet? Well, don't be. Just roll up your sleeves and get on it. It is a great idea to keep a spray bottle of disinfectant/antibacterial handy to keep your countertops and sink sanitary. *Always* use the disinfectant/antibacterial on your countertops and sink when they have come in contact with raw meat, eggs, chicken, or fish. Scrub your cutting boards and knives in hot soapy water or better yet, wash them in a hot dishwasher cycle.

And don't forget to wash your hands with soap and water while you're working in the kitchen, too.

## AREAS OF THE KITCHEN AND HOW TO CLEAN THEM:
**Garbage Disposal** – Is your garbage disposal not smelling so good? Toss in a couple of lemon slices and a couple of ice cubes with running water and grind it all up. It should smell better after this. You can toss in some citrus fruit slices or rinds to freshen it up any time.

**Oven** – The oven can be very dirty, but you can always close the door and turn out the light, right? Well, that only works for so long. Eventually it needs to be cleaned. If you have a self-cleaning oven, turn that on and let it do its job. Often after you use a self-cleaner, you will need to take a damp paper towel to wipe up the ash residue—after it cools, of course! It you do not have a self-cleaner, you can always use spray oven cleaners. They usually work well. You may need to take the baking racks out and wash them in the sink to clean them by hand. Use warm, soapy water and possibly even a scouring pad for these. Also, if you have some dried-on foods, sprinkle some baking soda on the spots and then scrub.

**Microwave** – How many times have you been in someone's relatively clean kitchen, only to be a bit grossed-out when you open their microwave? That's because, once again, spots and splatters can't hide when you open the door. A simple and easy way to clean the microwave is to heat two cups of water on high for five minutes. Let this hot water sit for five minutes, and everything in the microwave should be softened enough for you to easily wipe it off.

**Dishwasher –** Yes, even the dishwasher needs a little cleaning occasionally. If yours isn't cleaning the way you think it should, then you might consider giving it a once-over before calling the appliance repairman. You would be surprised at the things you will find in the bottom of your dishwasher. Pull out the racks and look around the drain. Being careful of broken pieces of glass or a small bone that could be hiding, clear away all particles that don't belong. Wipe around the rubber seal of the door to make sure nothing is standing in the way of a good, tight closure. Next, place a cup of white vinegar in a glass or cup right-side up on the top rack, and run through a hot water cycle. (Don't have anything else in the dishwasher during the vinegar cycle.)

**Refrigerator –** The refrigerator is another place where you can close the door and forget about it. That is, until you need a cold drink or you want to make a sandwich. To make sure nothing is lurking, rotting, or growing, begin by taking everything out, shelf by shelf. Throw out the food that has exceeded its expiration date. (You should also throw out food that has anything growing on it!) Wipe the shelves with warm, soapy water and dry them before you put the food back in. Do the same with the drawers. When you finish with the refrigerated side, open the freezer and do a cleaning there, too.

It is a great idea to place a fresh, open box of baking soda in each side. The baking soda will absorb odors. Step back, look inside, and enjoy the rewards of your work: a clean refrigerator.

**Garbage can –** Garbage cans don't have to smell; just because you throw garbage in doesn't mean that the container itself needs to be nasty. Begin by sprinkling some baking soda in the bottom of your garbage can. Then line your garbage can with bags that fit the size of your can. Always take the garbage out before it is overflowing. This will keep your kitchen cleaner, smelling better, and help to keep germs at bay.

**Toaster –** Toasters can get pretty icky if you don't clean them often. Breadcrumbs will accumulate in the bottom of the toaster, and these can scatter on your countertop when you move the toaster. There is a fairly easy solution to this. Unplug your toaster and take it over to the kitchen sink. Turn the toaster upside down with the open slots facing the sink and give it a few good shakes to empty the loose crumbs. Next, look underneath your toaster and slide the bottom covers off the toaster and wipe them off. Shake the toaster again to get the remaining crumbs out. Replace the bottom covers, wipe off the outside of your toaster, and toast away.

**Coffee maker** – Every so often you need to clean your coffee maker so that it will continue to make delicious, fresh-tasting coffee. Although some coffee maker manufacturers recommend a cleaning once a month, unless you are a real coffee connoisseur, every once in while should be good enough for yours. Cleaning a coffee maker is pretty simple. The rule is to fill your coffee pot or carafe with two parts water to one part vinegar. Pour the mixture into your water tank, turn on your machine, and run it through a brew cycle. It is a good idea to run two pots of clear water through after the vinegar mixture. After this, you should be good to go.

**Sinks** – Stainless steel sinks are the typical sink that people have these days. So if yours doesn't look so good, let's get it shiny again. Clean it with kitchen spray or a little bit of cleanser, rinse, and dry it well. Then use a small bit of orange oil, lemon oil, or baby oil and a soft cloth to help it retain its shine. To clean a ceramic sink, Mom recommends a product called Bar Keeper's Friend. It is non-abrasive and works very well on stains and scratches—pretty much a miracle worker. You can usually find it at your grocery or discount store.

**Drains** – To clean and freshen your kitchen drains, try the non-chemical approach. You will need baking soda and white vinegar. Pour ½ cup of baking soda down your drain. Next pour ½ cup of white vinegar. These two will begin a churning, bubbling action and will clean your drain without harmful chemicals.

## KITCHEN CLEANING CHECKLIST:

*Wipe down oven and burners on your stove, and remove any leftover food residue.
*Clean microwave.
*Check and clean appliances like dishwasher, refrigerator, toaster, and coffee maker.
*Clean and disinfect sinks and drains.
*Wipe down and dry all countertops and surfaces.
*Sweep/mop the floor.

## DON'T NEGLECT THE BATHROOM.

Bathrooms often get a bad rap for being the dirtiest or nastiest rooms in the house. But take heart, your bathroom doesn't have to fall into that category. You can decide right now to make sure that your bathroom stays clean. (It's no secret that Moms love clean bathrooms.) If you do a few simple things every day, your bathroom will not be a source of embarrassment (or mildew).

## BATHROOM CLEANING CHECKLIST:

☞ Keep wet towels picked up off the floor and hung up to dry for reuse.

☞ Use a daily shower cleaner after you finish to prevent mold and mildew growth.

☞ Place a toilet-cleaning disc in your toilet tank to keep it clean daily.

☞ Sweep or vacuum the floor, especially after drying your hair.

☞ Wipe your sink and countertop off with a hand towel after you finish your daily rituals.

☞ Replace caps on bottles and tubes to eliminate clutter.

☞ Keep a small squeegee in your shower to wipe down tile walls to prevent mildew.

**MOM-*sense*:** Out of paper towels and you still have glass and mirrors to clean? Use newspapers from that recycling stack in the hallway. They will do the trick.

**Make your bedroom a serene sanctuary (not a cluttered cave).** The bedroom is not typically the dirtiest room in your home, but it might be the most cluttered. Maybe this is because the bedroom is often the place where you drop everything that you don't want others to see. Primarily, you can keep your bedroom clean by keeping it picked up and clear of clothes and shoes. Get into the habit of putting things away in their specific place,

and when you do this, you won't have to worry about time-consuming cleaning. You will enjoy your room so much more if it is clean and inviting.

## BEDROOM CLEANING CHECKLIST:

◆ Make your bed and change your sheets weekly.

◆ Clear the room of clothes; put clean ones away and dirty ones in the laundry.

◆ Pick up all shoes and put them away.

◆ Clear the top of your chest of drawers or dresser, and put all loose and lost items away.

◆ Clear nightstand of unnecessary items.

◆ Check underneath the bed for anything that could have found its way there.

◆ Dust and polish all wood furniture.

◆ Wipe dust from photos and knick-knacks.

◆ Vacuum the carpet and rugs or clean the floor.

## MAKING A BED FROM BEGINNING TO END:

Clean-sheet night at Mom's house makes everybody happy. That's because nothing looks or feels better than a freshly changed and made bed. The feeling of clean sheets on a bed just makes you want to wrap up in the covers and snuggle in for a good night of sleep.

You will need a few items to make a bed look and feel good. You don't need to spend a small fortune, but you can still find good quality bedding if you shop around.

### Bed Necessities
*1 mattress pad*
*1 set of sheets (flat sheet and fitted sheet)*
*2 pillowcases or 1 for twin bed*
*1 blanket*
*1 bedspread or comforter*
*1 dust ruffle/bed skirt (if you desire)*

### 12 STEPS FOR MAKING A BED

**1**. If you are using a dust ruffle, this needs to go on first. Have someone help you lift the mattress off the box spring and onto the floor. Place the dust ruffle on, and then replace the mattress on top.

**2**. Cover your mattress with the mattress pad, stretching it tight and fitting it around the mattress corners snug.

**3**. Place your fitted sheet over the mattress pad and stretch it tightly over all four corners.

**4**. Lay your flat sheet, *wrong-side up,* flat on the mattress (I'll tell you why later).

**5**. Cover the flat sheet with your blanket, turning it wrong-side up as well.

**6**. At the foot of your bed, tuck in the flat sheet and blanket underneath the mattress beginning at the center of the mattress (leave the ends out for now), and do this the entire foot end/width of the mattress.

**7**. Now, lift the loose corner (on one side of the bed) of the sheet and blanket and pull it up onto the mattress, making a triangle shape.

**8**. Then tuck the leftover sheet/blanket left hanging underneath the mattress.

**9**. Pull the triangle of sheet/blanket back down and tuck it under the mattress for a neat looking bed.  (That's what we Moms call "hospital corners.")

**10**. Repeat with the other side of the bed.

**11**. Cover your bed with your bedspread or comforter. You can turn it down with your sheet and blanket laying neatly on top if you like.

**12**. Insert the pillows inside their pillowcases and place them at the head of your bed; step back and admire your handiwork!

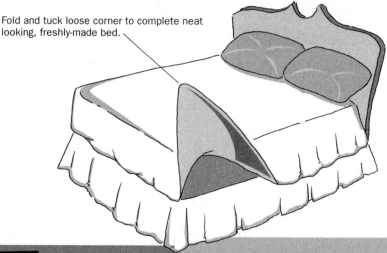

Fold and tuck loose corner to complete neat looking, freshly-made bed.

## HAVE A LIVING ROOM WORTH LIVING IN.

These areas can be you're easiest clean up or your hardest, depending upon how much stuff you drop at any given time. Plates and glasses seem to find resting places here, as well as clothes, shoes, magazines, and who knows what else. Mom knows that clutter can and should be managed on a daily basis to avoid massive cleaning time.

## LIVING ROOM/DEN CLEANING CHECKLIST:

❖ Remove all glasses, dishes, and food, and put them away.

❖ Neatly stack all magazines into a spot for later use.

❖ Organize CDs and DVDs.

❖ Remove all clothes lying on chairs, sofas, and the floor, and put them away.

❖ Remove all shoes, and put them away.

❖ Vacuum the floor and use an attachment to get underneath sofa and chair cushions, plus under the sofa and chairs.

❖ Dust and polish all wood furniture.

❖ Clean and shine glass-top furniture.

❖ Clean any glass doors leading in or out of this room.

❖ Clean the front and top of the television and/or audio equipment.

❖ Wipe off lampshades and lamps.

❖ Fluff pillows.

**Keep it sweet beneath your feet.** Surely you've heard the expression, "Her floors are clean enough to eat off of." I don't know about you, but Mom's never really had the urge to eat off anyone's floors. Your floors don't need to be clean enough for guests to eat spaghetti & meatballs on, but they should be clean enough to walk on or sit on.

Today, more than ever, we have a variety of flooring in almost every home, including apartments. Basically, the types boil down to carpet, hardwood or wood laminate, tile, and linoleum floorings. There are different ways for cleaning these different kinds of flooring surfaces, and they should be cleaned often to maintain their shine and durability.

### FLOOR CLEANING CHECKLIST:
#### Carpet
✓Vacuum thoroughly once a week.
✓Blot wet spills quickly to absorb the liquid with paper towels or a terry cloth towel.
✓Scrape solid residue or hardened spills with a dull knife.
✓For old stains, try pouring hydrogen peroxide on it. Cover the peroxide with a dampened towel.

If the stain is stubborn, place a hot iron on top of the towel for a few seconds.
✓Have your carpet steam-cleaned at least once a year.

#### Hardwood or wood laminate
✓Sweep or vacuum dirt and dust off the floor surface.
✓Using a damp mop (not dripping), clean the floors with plain water or water/vinegar mixture, using one part vinegar to one part warm water.

#### Tile
✓Sweep or vacuum dirt and dust away.
✓Mop once a week with ceramic tile floor cleaner or vinegar/water mixture using one gallon of water with only one cup of vinegar.

#### Linoleum
✓Sweep or vacuum dirt and dust away.
✓Mop with vinegar/water mixture using one gallon of warm/hot water with one cup of vinegar, or you can use a basic household cleaner diluted with warm/hot water.

### Don't forget to clean . . .
We've covered the main rooms, but these days, houses are filled with other nooks and crannies that need some attention as well.

## The Laundry Room

Even small rooms need a little attention every once in a while. This room will acquire mismatched socks, stuff from pants pockets, and probably a little junk, too. Try to keep this room organized so that you can actually get to the washing machine and dryer. Keep the floor clean and clear of too much excess stuff. Store your laundry detergent and cleaning products in cabinets, on shelves, or in a cart on the floor.

Remember to wipe clean the tops of your washing machine and dryer every couple of weeks because lint, dust, and dirt can accumulate here. Also, wipe clean the lid of the washing machine and the door of the dryer. While you are at it, go ahead and clean out the dispensers for bleach and fabric softener in your washing machine. If you have a hard time getting into the little crevices, try using a toothbrush.

If your washing machine is a little smelly and it just looks like it could use a good cleaning, run an empty laundry cycle using hot water, and then add two cups of white vinegar. This should clean your machine and rid it of any laundry detergent residue or dirt.

As I said before, make sure to *always* clean the lint trap of your dryer before every load. At least one time a year you should take the lint trap out of its holder and clean the space with your vacuum cleaner using a slim attachment. You'll be surprised just how much lint you will remove. Also, you should make sure that your dryer's exhaust pipe is correctly attached to the outdoor duct. Keeping your dryer clean and working properly can prevent fires.

One more thing . . . it won't hurt you to scoot your washing machine and dryer forward once a year and vacuum behind them. (Make it part of celebrating some obscure holiday!) It will be gross, but it will be clean when you finish!

## Outside your Front and Back Door

These spots can get a little dusty, cobwebs can spring up around them, and dirt can accumulate quickly. Wipe your door off and clean the glass if you have it. Wipe your light fixture with a little glass cleaner and paper towels. Change any burned out light bulbs. Buy an inexpensive doormat if you don't have one, and make your place look inviting and welcoming. There is nothing worse than a dirty doormat and cobwebs around a door to make someone think that they are spending an evening with the Addams family.

## ACCUMULATE SOME HANDY SKILLS.

*Handy* may not be the word to describe you, but *capable* sure can be. Everyone, including petite females, is capable of doing basic repairs around the home. You don't

**Toolbox** that contains a hammer, needle-nose pliers, flat screwdriver, Phillips-head screwdriver, tape measure, adjustable wrench, socket wrench, hexagonal driver, and a level

**Hardware** such as picture hangers, nails, an assortment of screws, duct tape, electrical tape, and masking tape

**Extras around the house** such as batteries for remotes and such (AA and AAA); plunger for commodes and sinks (keep in an easy-to-find place); filters for your air conditioning and heating units (1–2 months' worth)

need to call a handyman to do basic repairs or hang your pictures on the walls. You can do most all household repairs without spending a fortune. Hardware and home improvement stores all have employees on hand that can answer your questions and give advice. Don't be afraid to tackle a job by yourself—just make sure you are equipped and you have done your homework.

# J.A.M. Session: A little Q and A with MOM

**What can I do about makeup stains in my bathroom sink?**
Try pouring a little hydrogen peroxide on them to loosen for easier clean up.

**How do I clean my camera lens on my cell phone?**
Use a Q-tip swab and a small amount of alcohol. Gently wipe the lens clean in a circular motion. Your next photo won't look so cloudy.

**Oops! What can I do about a nasty ink stain on my countertop?**
Don't worry, just pour a bit of rubbing alcohol on it, and it should dissolve and just wipe away!

### How do I clean up spilled candle wax?

Ah, the old stubborn candle wax problem. Here's what you do: let the wax harden, and scrape it off with a dull knife, or even try a credit card. If the wax has spilled on fabric or carpet, place a paper towel over the wax and use a warm iron, gliding it across the towel in a back-and-forth motion. It should transfer to the towel.

### How do I clean mini-blinds?

Try using a dryer sheet that has been dampened with water. Close the blinds in one direction and wipe them clean from top to bottom. The dryer sheet should help reduce the static that gathers the dust.

### What's the best way to clean picture frames?

To prevent damaging the photos, clean them gently. Spray glass cleaner onto a paper towel and wipe the glass clean. Never spray the cleaner directly onto the glass in the frame, because it could seep behind the glass and damage your photo.

### How do I get rid of mildew on my shower curtain?

Don't throw it out if it is still in good shape. Toss it in the washing machine on a hot water cycle with your regular detergent and a capful of bleach. Add a white or light-colored towel to the wash to agitate and scrub the mildew off. Hang to dry.

## Just one more thing . . .

⋆ **Don't forget to clean the top of the blades of your ceiling fans.** They get very dusty and can scatter dust when your fan runs. Try using the Swiffer-type dusters because they fold at a 90-degree angle and allow you to easily clean the fan blades. (And watch out for falling dustbunnies!)

⋆ **Every so often, remove glass ceiling light fixtures and clean them.** They are usually easy to remove by merely turning a screw or two. Shake them clean of bugs and dust over the garbage can, and wipe them clean or wash them in warm, soapy water. Otherwise, you may look up and find a cemetery for bugs.

⋆ **Remember your filters.** Change your air-conditioning and heating filters once a month to ensure that your unit will run properly, and to keep your air cleaner.

⋆ **Shut, then flush.** Always close the toilet lid before you flush it. Spray can occur, and that is just plain unpleasant.

⋆ **To get rid of some common smelly odors:**
*Bathroom Odors* – Light a candle or promptly strike a match.
*Burned popcorn* – First, take the popcorn outside your home, then light a candle.
*Onion or garlic on your hands* – Rub lemon juice on them.

# CHAPTER FOUR

# Stocking the Kitchen

*"If you can read, you can cook."*

A good cook I know used to say the above phrase whenever someone complimented her cooking. I agree with her. Sure, it's true that some of us have more talent in the kitchen than others, but it's also true that anybody can learn to cook. It just takes a little time and practice. And with all the ready-made ingredients that are available and today's Food Channel and the Internet offering nonstop advice, you're a step ahead of where Mom was when she started out.

It is doubtful that your kitchen looks like Emeril's—unless you have a nice trust fund. Let's face it, most first kitchens come equipped with lots of lovingly-used donations from Mom: mismatched silverware, old skillets, used Tupperware, and lots of inexpensive purchases from the local discount store. The truth is, that is okay! Most of us don't start out with the best of everything. And you don't have to be outfitted with the finest commercial appliances or the most expensive pots and pans to learn to cook. But you will need some basic items to begin your foray into the culinary world. This is what we Moms call "stocking the kitchen."

# MOM'S REQUIRED INGREDIENTS FOR A WELL-STOCKED STARTER KITCHEN

## FOR THE STOVETOP:

✗One small skillet and one large skillet with lid (non-stick is your best bet; stainless steel is great)

✗One small and one large saucepan with lids (for cooking most everything)

✗Large stockpot with lid (for pastas and soups)

✗A whistling tea pot (if you like hot beverages)

## BAKING AND OVENWARE:

✓Cookie sheet (Mom loves the air-bake—no burned cookies here!)

✓9 x 13 baking pan

✓8 x 8 baking pan (or a 9 x 9 size)

✓Pizza pan

✓Loaf pan

✓8- or 9-inch pie pan

✓Muffin tin (for muffins and cupcakes)

## TOOLS, GADGETS, AND ESSENTIALS:

✳4 to 6 kitchen towels and dishwashing cloths

✳2 to 3 pot holders and 1 oven mitt

✳Liquid measuring cup (the 2-cup size is best and can go in the microwave)

✳Dry measuring cups

✳Measuring spoons

✳Cutting board (the synthetic kind doesn't hold bacteria like wood and can go in the dishwasher for sanitizing)

✳2 or 3 good knives (4-inch paring knife, 6- or 8-inch serrated knife, and a 10-inch chef's knife should handle most of your needs)

✳Kitchen scissors (wonderful for cutting chicken and some vegetables)

✳Mixing bowls that stack (2 or 3 of different sizes)

✳Wooden spoons of different lengths (great because they don't hold heat, so you won't burn your hand)

✳A wire whisk (for eggs, pancake and cake batters, whipped cream, and meringues)

✳Tongs (for moving hot foods the safe way)

✳Pasta server

✳A couple of heat resistant rubber spatulas

✳A colander and wire mesh strainer (for draining and straining everything)

✳A salad spinner (for cleaning lettuces, it is a fabulous thing!)

✳A flat spatula/turner/flipper (for serving, lifting, and flipping food)

✳A meat thermometer

✳A grater (box-type or flat)

✳A corkscrew

✳A bottle opener

✳An ice cream scoop

✳A can opener (manual or electric)

✳Salt and pepper shakers (a pepper mill is great if you like fresh pepper)

✳A 2-quart pitcher with lid

✳A small fire extinguisher (just in case)

✳3 to 4 ice cube trays (if you don't have an ice maker)

✳Plastic containers with lids (the stackable kind at the grocery store are great for leftovers)

✳Garbage can

## First things first: Start off small.

Stocking your kitchen with the necessities doesn't mean spending so much on cookware that you can't afford the food to cook in it. Williams-Sonoma and Viking can wait: buy what you can afford. Many of the large discount stores today have great items that are inexpensive, but good quality; shop around.

### SMALL APPLIANCES THAT MAKE LIFE MUCH EASIER:

- A blender
- A coffee maker
- An electric hand mixer
- A food processor
- A microwave
- A toaster oven

## Go shopping!

Now that you've got your kitchen in order, it's time to stock that pantry and refrigerator. Ask around for the best places to shop for groceries; whether you are in a city, suburb, or more rural area, there are local favorites. In a nod to convenience, most people tend to choose the store closest to them.

## TIPS FOR SAVVY GROCERY SHOPPING

**1. Never go grocery shopping when you are hungry.**
Mom knows that this is the first rule of grocery shopping. If you ignore this and shop while your stomach is growling, you will find your cart is filled with everything from Cheetos to fudge ice cream because everything looks so good!

**2. Make a list before you go.**
If you a planning a meal or you just need a few things, chances are you will forget something. Moms have learned this the hard way.

**3. Buy leaner cuts of meat.**
Today's shopper has a wide variety of choices, from 85 percent lean beef to ground turkey and chicken. Dare to try the leaner cuts, as they are so much healthier for you.

**4. Never start shopping in the frozen food aisle or the cold food aisle.** Save these for the end and eliminate runny ice cream!

**5. Compare prices and don't buy the first thing you pick up.**
Just because an item is stacked and featured on the end of the aisle *does not* mean it's on sale. The store may just have a huge surplus it needs to unload.

**6. Clip and use coupons.** Frugal Moms have saved many dollars by cutting out coupons in the weekly circular, especially when the coupon is used on an item that's already on sale. But don't buy something you won't use just because you have a coupon.

**7. Buy fresh fruits and vegetables when they are in season.**
They will be less expensive, more delicious than canned or frozen, and so much better for you. (Check out a local Farmer's Market for the best locally grown produce. It's lots of fun!)

**8. Understand before buying that organic and chemical free foods will probably be more expensive.**
This is unfortunate, but true.

**9. Keep an eye on the prices as your groceries are scanned at the checkout.**
Occasionally, the price will ring up wrong, and some stores will make concessions for that. There is always the chance that an item which scans higher than priced will be given to you for free.

## STOCK THE PANTRY.

Welcome to the wonderful world of canned and baking goods, perishables and non-perishables! Your first big trip to the supermarket may be a little overwhelming, but remember, some of these items will last months and even years—that salt you're picking up will flavor countless meals ahead.

### NON-PERISHABLE ITEMS

All-purpose flour

Baking soda

Bread

Canned soup

Canned tomatoes

Canned tomato sauce

Canned tuna

Canned vegetables and fruit

Cereal

Chicken stock

Coffee/Tea

Crackers

Honey

Jam/Jelly

Non-stick cooking spray

Olive oil

Pasta

Peanut butter

Popcorn

Rice

Soy sauce

Sugar

Vinegar

Worcestershire sauce

## NON-EDIBLE ITEMS

Aluminum foil

Dishwashing liquid and/or
dishwasher detergent

Garbage bags

Napkins

Paper towels

Paper plates

Parchment paper (for use
on cookie sheets to
prevent burning)

Plastic wrap

Wax paper

Zipper-type plastic bags

## PERISHABLE ITEMS FOR THE REFRIGERATOR OR FREEZER

Butter

Cheese

Eggs

Frozen vegetables*

Ketchup

Lemons

Mayonnaise

Milk

Mustard

Onions

Parmesan cheese

*Broccoli, carrots, corn, peas, and
spinach are good choices—they
keep well and can be thawed and
added to many recipes.*

**MOM-*sense*:** Take a peek
inside the egg carton before you
buy them. If you see one that's
cracked, put that case back and
get another one. Cracked eggs can
carry bacteria.

## SPICES AND SEASONINGS

**Basic pantry stockers:**

Basil

Bay leaves

Black pepper

Chili powder

Cinnamon

Curry powder

Dry mustard

Garlic powder

Ginger

Kosher salt (for cooking)

Nutmeg

Onion flakes

Oregano

Paprika

Parsley flakes

Rosemary

Salt (iodized)

Thyme

Vanilla extract

**Later, you can add these to your pantry as needed:**

Cayenne pepper

Chives

Cilantro flakes

Cloves

Dill weed

Mace

Marjoram

Peppermint

Saffron

Sage

Savory

Tarragon

Turmeric

*Tomatoes and oregano*

*make it Italian;*

...............

*Wine and tarragon*

*make it French.*

...............

*Sour cream makes it Russian;*

...............

*Lemon and cinnamon*

*make it Greek.*

...............

*Soy sauce makes it Chinese;*

...............

*Garlic makes it good.*

**—ALICE MAY BROCK**

## GET ACQUAINTED WITH HERBS AND SPICES.

When I first started to cook, I was a little afraid to experiment with all the seasonings I had bought, even though they were just inside the door of the cupboard. Slowly, I overcame my fears and began adding some spice to foods. I have never looked back! Don't ever be afraid to give a little shake to a piece of meat or to vegetables to enhance their flavor; spices and herbs can make all the difference between bland and delicious food. (Key phrase: "little shake"; Mom has learned that there can be too much of a good thing.)

### Herbs

Herbs are typically the leaves of plants used in dry or fresh form. While fresh herbs definitely are more flavorful, dry herbs in the form of whole, crushed, or ground are often more readily available and affordable. If you choose to purchase fresh, store them in the refrigerator, preferably wrapped in a damp paper towel and placed in a plastic bag.

### Spices

Spices come from the bark (cinnamon), berry (black pepper), buds (cloves), fruit (paprika), root (garlic, ginger, onion), and seeds (yellow mustard) of tropical plants and trees. Spices can entice you with their aromatic fragrances and can add just the right "kick" or flavor to a dish.

### Dehydrated Vegetable Seasonings

There are many dehydrated vegetable seasonings on the market. The choices will often include chives, garlic, mint, sweet pepper, and onion. Dehydrated vegetable seasonings can be used on meats, in soups and salad dressings, and shaken on vegetables to add extra flavor.

### Condiments

Condiments are herbs and spices that are blended and served in liquid form. Common types are ketchup, mustard, steak sauce, Tabasco sauce, and Worcestershire sauce. I'm sure you don't need any advice on how to use them!

## Common Herbs and Spices and their uses:

**Basil** has a mint-like, sweet scent and taste. Although often used to enhance Italian recipes and tomato sauces, basil can also add much to sandwiches, fish, and poultry. It blends well with oregano, thyme, and garlic.

**Bay Leaves** have a bitter, sharp taste and can be pungent. Bay leaves add great flavor to homestyle and hearty cooking, like stews, soups, vegetables, and roasts. *Place the whole bay leaf in the recipe while cooking, but remove them before serving.*

**Black Pepper**, the common table condiment, has a pungent, sharp flavor. Use black pepper to kick up marinades and sauces or sprinkle it over soups, eggs, and vegetables. Pepper can be used on almost anything.

**Chili Powder** is a mix of spices including dried ground chile peppers, cumin, garlic, and oregano. Chili powder is used to spice up chili, of course, but is also used in many other dishes, including Mexican and beef.

**Cinnamon** has a sweet, woody fragrance, and comes in both ground and stick forms. As perhaps the most commonly used baking spice, cinnamon is frequently found in desserts and fruit recipes. In the Middle East, it is even used in chicken and lamb dishes.

**MOM-*sense*:** Here's a little secret—cinnamon is a great accompaniment to chocolate.

**Curry Powder** is a blend of spices commonly used in Indian and Asian foods. Curry can be used in marinades for meats, in egg dishes, and also adds flavor to dips and sauces.

**Dry Mustard** has no aroma when dry, but a hot flavor is released when it's mixed with water to form a paste. It is great in salad dressings when used with oil and vinegar because it helps them blend and adds a little zip. Dry mustard can also be used with meats, fish, and vegetables.

**Garlic Powder** has a distinctive flavor and odor. Garlic powder is great when used in marinades and can be rubbed on meats to season before cooking.

**Garlic Salt** is just that: garlic powder and salt combined. You can use garlic salt in many of the same ways as garlic powder, just be mindful of the salt and don't add more.

**Ginger** carries a rich, sweet, and warm aroma but has a bite and can be a bit hot. Ginger is used in many Asian recipes and is found in ginger ale, gingerbread, spice cake, and cookies.

**Kosher Salt** is a larger grained salt than regular table salt. Kosher salt is used primarily for cooking. Use Kosher salt when salting boiling water for pastas and vegetables. *Kosher salt does not contain iodine.*

**Nutmeg** is sweet smelling and pungent. Ground nutmeg is a great baking spice and is as a topping when sprinkled over eggnog, custard, and whipped cream. It can also be used on vegetables, fish, or chicken. (Guess what popular sauce has a hint of this spice? You got it—Alfredo!)

**Onion Flakes** can be as flavorful as fresh onions when rehydrated and added to liquids such as soups or marinades.

**Oregano** has a very pungent odor. It is a fabulous accent for pasta dishes and salad dressings. Oregano is what gives pizza sauce its great flavor.

**Paprika** comes from mild red peppers, so it can range from sweet to hot. Paprika is often used as a garnish for vegetable dishes, casseroles, and stuffed eggs. It can be used on any savory dish.

**Parsley Flakes** have a light, fresh scent and flavor. Parsley flakes can be added to cooked foods, melted butter, and salad dressings for a light touch.

MOM-*sense*: Parsley is a great breath freshener.

**Rosemary** is very aromatic and has a bold flavor. Use rosemary in chicken, lamb, and pork dishes. Also try it in tomato-based recipes.

**Salt (Iodized)** is table salt that has been mixed with a small amount of sodium iodide. This helps to prevent iodine deficiency in people, which can lead to thyroid gland issues. You will want to buy iodized salt for your saltshakers.

**Thyme** has a minty and somewhat lemony aroma. Thyme is great in

## BLENDED SEASONINGS THAT CAN PROVIDE INSTANT FLAVOR

The following seasonings combine several spices to give you a boost of flavor.

**Cajun Seasoning** – Gives a spicy kick to your foods. Add to coatings or directly onto chicken, fish, and meats.

**Italian Seasoning** – A great blend of the thyme, oregano, basil, sage, and marjoram. Simply a great addition to any Italian dish.

**Jerk Seasoning** – Adds a little Caribbean flair to your food. Sprinkle on your chicken, fish, or meats for tropical flavor.

**Mexican Seasoning** – Great on meat for tacos, fajitas, enchiladas, or other Mexican dishes.

**Old Bay Seasoning** – Fabulous for seafood of any kind. Perfect when added to the water of boiled shrimp, lobster, or crabs. Can sprinkle on any seafood before cooking.

---

pizza and spaghetti sauces, as well as rubbed on chicken, pork, or beef.

**Vanilla Extract** has a perfumed, sweet aroma. Vanilla extract is very popular when used to flavor desserts and drinks. It can also be used to balance sauces for chicken and shellfish. Moms prefer *Pure Vanilla Extract* and not imitation.

## KNOW ABOUT QUALITY AND QUANTITY OF FRESH FOODS.

All the spices and herbs in the world are useless without what we Moms like to call "perishables"(you know, the food that goes bad and doesn't come in a cereal box). Now it's time to buy some *real food*—fresh fruits and vegetables, meats, cheeses, and dairy products. And since this cooking thing is new, you might be a little confused about how much to buy. Grocery shopping can be expensive, and you certainly don't want to buy too much food only to have it spoil. Wasting food is not a good thing, surely your Mom told you that!

## WHEN A RECIPE CALLS FOR THIS, I NEED THIS

Apples, *3 c. sliced or chopped* = 3 medium apples

Bacon, *½ c. crumbled* = 8 slices of cooked bacon

Butter, *½ c.* = 1 stick or ¼ pound butter

Celery, *1 c. chopped* = 2 stalks of celery

Cheese, *2 c. grated* = 1/2 lb. (8 oz.) cheese

Chicken, *2 c. cooked and diced* = 2 chicken breasts

Chocolate chips, *2 c.* = 1 6 oz. package

Corn, *1 c. kernels* = 2 ears of corn

Green pepper, *1 c. diced* = 1 large pepper

Hamburger or turkey, *2 c. crumbled* = 1 lb. beef or turkey

Lemon juice, *2–3 T.* = 1 medium lemon

Lettuce, *6 c. torn* = 1 head of lettuce

Nuts, *1 c. chopped* = 1/4 lb. nuts

Onion, *1 c. chopped* = 2 medium or 1 large onion

Potatoes, *2 c., cooked and cubed* = 3 medium potatoes

Rice, *3 c. cooked* = 1 c. uncooked rice

Spaghetti, *4 c. cooked* = 7 ounces uncooked spaghetti

Strawberries, *2 c. sliced* = 1 pint of strawberries

Sugar, brown *2 1/3 c.* = 1 lb. (16 oz.) brown sugar

Sugar, granulated *2 c.* = 1 lb. (16 oz.) sugar

Sugar, powdered *3 ½ c.* = 1 lb. (16 oz.) powdered sugar

**MOM-*sense*:** Here's a fabulous seasoning mix to keep on hand. I must give a nod to one of my favorite Southern cooks, Paula Deen, for this one. Combine 1 cup of salt, ¼ cup of garlic powder, and ¼ cup of black pepper, and use on just about everything. Paula calls this her house seasoning, and it has become mine as well. I keep mine in a Parmesan cheese shaker and keep it in my pantry with my other herbs and spices. It is fabulous on everything, so give it a try. When you grow to love it and share the tip with your friends, give the credit to Paula.

## CHOOSING FRUITS AND VEGETABLES

When you are shopping for fruits, look for tender, plump, and brightly colored fruits. Fruits should be firm when held in your hand. Don't buy fruits that are mushy, bruised, moldy, or showing signs of mildew. (Exception: Overripe bananas for Mom's Banana Bread!) Some fruits will be too firm because they were picked before they were completely ripe. It is okay to buy these, but know that they are not ready to eat just yet. Place the firm fruit in a dark corner of your kitchen to continue the ripening process for a day or so, or place it in a paper bag and keep at room temperature. Check on it daily.

The same rules apply for vegetables as far as buying the best-looking choices. Remember to wash them before you use them. Many foods today have been sprayed with pesticides, and even though they are washed before you buy them, you should *always* wash them at home, too. Your Mom doesn't want you getting sick!

| FRUITS | HOW TO PICK | HOW TO STORE |
|--------|-------------|--------------|
| Apples | Firm, good color | Refrigerate |
| Avocados | Dark, firm | Refrigerate |
| Bananas | Yellow or green | Room temperature until ripe (yellow) |
| Berries | Firm, solid, plump | Refrigerate, watch for mold |
| Cantaloupe | Stem end should be a little soft | Room temperature until cut, then refrigerate |
| Grapefruit | Thin skin, avoid thick | Room temperature or refrigerate |
| Grapes | Plump, no bruises | Refrigerate (great snack when frozen, too!) |
| Honeydew | Firm, pale yellow or white; avoid soft | Room temperature until cut, then refrigerate |
| Kiwi | Firm and not soft | Brown bag on the counter |

| | | |
|---|---|---|
| Lemons | Firm, thin skin, not thick | Refrigerate 2–3 weeks |
| Limes | Dark better than pale | Refrigerate 2–3 weeks |
| Oranges | Firm; green tint okay | Refrigerate 2–3 weeks |
| Peaches | Ripe should be soft to touch; deep color, avoid green | Brown bag on counter |
| Pears | Firm, but soft at stem | Room temperature |
| Pineapple | Plump with sweet smell; leaves should pull out easily | Room temperature until cut |
| Plums | Firm, plump, not soft or wrinkled | Room temperature if needs to ripen, then refrigerate |
| Tomatoes | Plump, well shaped, firm | Room temperature |
| Watermelon | Smooth, round, not shiny | Refrigerate or room temperature |

| VEGETABLES | HOW TO PICK | HOW TO STORE |
|---|---|---|
| Artichokes | Small, tightly closed | Refrigerate, don't let get tough |
| Asparagus | Firm, straight, tender stalks; not too big or long | Refrigerate in covered container |
| Beans | Crisp, bright-colored | Refrigerate in covered container |
| Broccoli | Firm, tight heads; not yellow | Refrigerate in covered container |
| Cabbage | Firm, heavy; no holes | Refrigerate in covered container |

| | | |
|---|---|---|
| **Carrots** | Bright orange, straight, and not too thick | Refrigerate in plastic bag |
| **Cauliflower** | White, not brown, heavy | Refrigerate in covered container |
| **Celery** | Crisp ribs, good green color | Refrigerate |
| **Corn** | If pierced, liquid squirts from kernel (check for worms) | Refrigerate with husks on |
| **Cucumbers** | Firm, no soft spots | Refrigerate |
| **Eggplant** | Plump, glossy, heavy; deep purple | Refrigerate 2–3 days |
| **Lettuce** | Heavy, good green color; not wilted | Refrigerate in zippered bag |
| **Mushrooms** | Firm, plump, not shriveled | Refrigerate unwashed |
| **Onions** | Firm, full, no blemishes | Room temperature |
| **Peppers** | Bright colors, good shape; not shriveled | Refrigerate covered |
| **Potatoes** | Clean, smooth, good color; not green or shriveled | Cool, dry, dark place |
| **Spinach** | Crisp, dry | Wash in cold water and dry. Refrigerate in storage container with a paper towel. |
| **Sweet Potatoes** | Small, smooth, firm | Cool, dry, dark place |
| **Zucchini and Summer Squash** | Firm, free of cuts, small, tender | Refrigerate |

Your pantry is full. The pans are gleaming. You've stacked your dishes, stocked your refrigerator, wiped your counters, and arranged your spices just so. Stand back and survey the warmth of your kitchen. Ahhhhh!

All stocked up and ready to go? Okay, now it's time to get cooking!

## ACQUIRE A FEW GOOD COOKBOOKS.

Cooking is basically experimentation by trial and error. You will make mistakes—everyone does—but you will learn from them and hopefully won't repeat them too often.

I would advise everyone to copy some of your mother's, grandmother's, aunt's, sister's, and favorite cook's recipes before you move out on your own. You'll want that recipe for Mom's Chicken Soup, Aunt Edna's Apple Pie, or Sophie's Lasagna someday, so why not copy them now while you are young and have the energy? You can buy a recipe box to store notecards in, write them in a special journal, or you can do the 3-ring binder method and copy them on notebook paper or print them off on your computer. I have also seen a great little blank cookbook that allows you to fill in with the recipes you collect. You won't regret the time you spend saving these heirloom treasures!

Mom also recommends buying one or two good cookbooks to get started. It will be money well spent. Your own Mother might even choose to pass one of her favorite books along to you. If so, treasure its flour-stained pages.

**MOM-*sense*:** Some of my very favorite cookbooks are the locally published kind from churches and women's groups. They are usually terrific.

**Some cookbooks MOM recommends:**
*The Way to Cook* by Julia Child
*The Barefoot Contessa Cookbook* by Ina Garten
*Everyday Food/Great Food Fast* from The Kitchens of Martha Stewart Living
*Rachael Ray's 30-Minute Get Real Meals* by Rachael Ray
*Better Homes and Gardens New Cook Book* by Better Homes and Gardens Books
*Everyday Italian* by Giada De Laurentiis

If you choose to purchase a cookbook, or if you beg off some family recipes, I encourage you to read them. I mean *really* read them before you get ready to try a recipe. Make yourself familiar with the ingredients and the description of preparation. There's nothing like being in the middle of a recipe only to realize you don't have that teaspoon of celery salt that it calls for—or that you added *all* of the butter when half of it was supposed to go on top! (That's what that little word, *divided*, means by the way—you split up an ingredient and add it at different times.)

The Internet also offers many opportunities to find great recipes. You can search for just about anything, and most of the time you will discover many choices. Some of Mom's favorite sites are allrecipes.com, myrecipes.com, epicurious.com, and foodnetwork.com.

As you begin your culinary adventure, pick some basic recipes to start out. (Mom will be glad to help!) This will help you become accustomed to your appliances and your kitchen's flow and layout. *Please don't begin with the most difficult recipe in the book.* We don't all start out with Baked Alaska or Coquille St. Jacques. It took all Moms years to get where we are. Take your time and learn. Cooking, like most things, improves with practice and patience.

**MOM-*sense*:** When you are ready to cook a recipe with several ingredients, prepare them first and keep them separated until you are ready to combine them. Do your chopping, slicing, measuring, and cutting before you begin cooking.

## COMMON RECIPE ABBREVIATIONS

| | |
|---|---|
| **teaspoon(s)** | tsp. or t. |
| **tablespoon(s)** | Tbsp. or T. |
| **cup** | c. |
| **pint** | pt. |
| **quart** | qt. |
| **gallon** | gal. |
| **ounce** | oz. |
| **pound** | lb. |
| **minute** | min. |
| **hour** | hr. |

## LEARN HOW TO MEASURE INGREDIENTS.

Mom doesn't keep all those different types of spoons and measuring cups in her cabinet just for fun. To make sure everything comes *out* of the oven all right, it helps to put it *in* right in the first place!

Here's how to measure some common ingredients:

*Baking powder, baking soda, salt, pepper, spices, and herbs:* Fill measuring spoon until it overflows, and using the dull side of a knife, level it off.

*Flour, powdered sugar, and granulated sugar:* Fill the dry measuring cup (usually metal or plastic) until it overflows. Tap the cup slightly with your hand to help the flour or sugar settle inside the cup. Add more if necessary. Using the dull side of a knife, level it off. (If your recipe calls for sifted flour or powdered sugar, sift before measuring.)

*Brown sugar:* Pack the sugar tightly into the measuring cup using a spoon. Continue to pack the sugar until it is level with the top of the cup.

*Liquids, including milk and water:* Use a liquid measuring cup (usually glass or clear plastic) that is sitting on a level surface, pour the liquid to the correct level.

## GET FAMILIAR WITH COOKING TERMS.

Specific directions for different recipes can be confusing—especially if you haven't been to culinary school lately. Never fear. Cooking terms can be easily learned (or Googled), but you need to pay attention to their meanings so you will follow the right procedures when cooking. (Think how impressed your friends will be when you bring up dredging, braising, and parboiling in casual conversation!)

## Common Cooking Terms:

**Bake** – To cook food in an oven, surrounded by dry heat.

**Baste** – To brush or spoon liquid over food as it cooks; usually melted butter, or meat drippings.

**Blanch** – To plunge food briefly into boiling water, and then remove it and place directly into cold water. One use of blanching is to remove the skin from tomatoes or peaches.

**Boil** – To cook in a liquid that has bubbles rising and breaking the surface. The temperature is 212 degrees.

**Braise** – To brown meat in oil quickly and then cook it in a pan that is covered either in the oven or on top of the stove.

**Broil** – To cook food just below direct heat. Use a pan when broiling in your oven.

**Chill** – To cool foods either in the refrigerator or freezer. You can also place food on ice for quick chilling.

**Chop** – To cut foods with a knife into small pieces.

**Cream** – To mix together until the mixture is smooth and creamy. Usually, you will cream sugar with butter or shortening.

**Devein** – To remove the black gritty vein that runs down the top of shrimp. Do this by running a paring knife over the skin to slit it, and pull out the vein. *Yes, it's gross, but you'll get used to it.*

**Dice** – To cut food into small cubes, roughly the same size.

**Dredge** – To coat meat with a dry ingredient like flour, cornmeal, or breadcrumbs before cooking.

**Fold** – To add an ingredient to a mixture that has already been mixed. Slowly, add the new ingredient to the center of the mixture and stir from the bottom of the bowl upward to incorporate everything together.

**Fry** – *Pan Fry:* to cook in a small amount of fat or oil. *Deep Fry:* to cook in fat or oil that completely covers the food being cooked.

**Glaze** – A coating that is applied to food by drizzling, spooning, or brushing. Glazes will often harden and add shine to foods.

**Grate** – To take a large piece of food and reduce it to small particles by rubbing it against a grater that is coarse and serrated. *Be careful not to grate your fingers too!*

**Marinate** – To cover food with a marinade so that it will have more flavor. Marinades typically contain oil and/or vinegar. *Always refrigerate and cover food that is marinating.*

**Mince** – To cut food into very fine pieces, much smaller than chopped.

**Mix** – To stir two or more ingredients together by hand or to beat with an electric mixer until they are combined thoroughly.

**Parboil** – To cook food very briefly in boiling liquid before cooking it another way. *It is a good idea to parboil chicken before grilling it because it lessens your chances of burning the chicken and assures you that the chicken will be cooked thoroughly.*

**Poach** – To cook food in a simmering liquid, not boiling. The food should not fall apart.

**Puree** – To change food from a solid form to a smooth, easily spreadable consistency by using a blender or a food processor.

**Roast** – To cook by dry heat in an oven. Usually you will roast meats uncovered.

**Sauté** – To cook or brown food quickly, typically in butter or oil. *When you sauté onions, their color will change to clear or translucent.*

**Score** – To cut slits into the surface, usually the center, of food for decorative purposes, to tenderize it, or to keep the edges from curling up. *Often you will score a ham if you plan to glaze it.*

**Sear** – A quick way to brown meat to seal in the juices before you continue cooking it in another form. Searing requires a small amount of butter or oil.

**Simmer** – To cook food that doesn't reach a rapid boil. Do this over medium or low heat.

**Steam** – A way to cook with indirect heat over boiling water. Typically you will place a bamboo steam basket or a steamer pan over a pan of water. Cover your pan and the steam will cook the food. *You can also place vegetables in a shallow dish with a very small amount of water, cover with plastic wrap and microwave for 4–5 minutes. Check for doneness, season to taste, and enjoy.*

**Steep** – To let food sit in water that has just reached the boiling point in order to achieve the maximum amount of flavor. *Allow tea bags* to steep in hot water for at least 5 minutes, covered, to have the best flavor.

**Stir** – To combine ingredients with a spoon, not a mixer.

**Thickening Agent** – Flour is the most common. Use 2 T. flour with 1 cup of liquid to thicken. Flour is used in gravies and sauces. Cornstarch is another thickening agent that can thicken for a translucent look in glazes and sauces. Use 1 T. cornstarch with 1 cup of liquid.

**Toss** – To mix or combine ingredients with two utensils by lifting and dropping over and over.

**Whip** – To beat a food quickly to add air into it so that the volume increases and it becomes lighter. Use a wire whisk or an electric mixer.

**Be ready to improvise. (Emergency Substitutions!)**

Okay, so you've planned your meal, been to the grocery, invited your guests, and now you're ready to cook. Alas, you don't have a couple of the ingredients listed on the recipe. Your neighbor isn't home to borrow from. Now what do you do?

Don't panic—though it's best to use what's called for, there are ways to get around some ingredients. Hopefully what you're missing is listed here, and you will be able to prepare that delicious recipe after all. (If not, that's why they invented delivery pizza!)

### OH NO, I DON'T HAVE IT!
The recipe calls for **this** . . . I'll use **that** instead

Bread crumbs, seasoned, 1 c. = 3 slices bread (finely ground) + 1 t. pepper

Buttermilk, ½ c. = ½ c. milk + 1 ½ t. vinegar

Chili beans, 8 oz. can = 8 oz. can kidney beans + 2 t. chili powder

Corn starch (for thickening), 1 T. = 2 T. flour

Dry mustard, 1 t. = 1 t. yellow prepared mustard

Garlic, 1 clove = ⅛ t. garlic powder

Herbs, 1 T. fresh = 1 t. dried

Ketchup, ½ c. = ½ c. tomato sauce + 1 T. vinegar and 1 c. sugar

Mushrooms, fresh, ½ lb. = 4 oz. can mushrooms

Onion, 1 c. chopped = ⅓ c. onion flakes

Parsley, fresh, 1 T. = 1 t. parsley flakes

Ricotta cheese, 1 c. = 1 c. cottage cheese + 1 T. skim milk

Self-rising flour, 1 c. = 1 c. plain flour +1 t. baking powder and ½ t. salt

Whipping cream, 1 c. = ¾ c. milk + ½ c. butter

## LEARN TO APPRECIATE OUR FRIEND, VINEGAR.

I know what you're thinking. "Vinegar is weird, stinky stuff with an even weirder name." Well, vinegar is really more valuable than weird; in fact, you won't believe how many ways you can use it. Besides, vinegar has been a household staple of Moms for generations, so it can't be that bad. *Don't be afraid of vinegar.* It is an essential ingredient in many recipes and is a favorite component of several home remedies and cleaning solutions. With a little vinegar, you can remove stains, clean your floors, and then, presto! whip up a fast vinaigrette salad dressing.

Simply put, vinegar is a solution of water and acetic acid (fermented liquid from wine, beer, apple cider, fruit juice, etc.). Vinegar can be kept in the pantry and doesn't need to be refrigerated. White vinegar can be kept for a very long time, but other kinds are good for only about six months after opening.

## BASIC TYPES OF AND USES FOR VINEGAR

**Balsamic Vinegar** – made in Italy. Balsamic vinegar is made from grapes and is aged for three to twelve years. Dark brown in color, its taste is a mix of sweet and sour. Balsamic vinegar is used for marinades, sauces, gravies, and vinaigrette salad dressings.

**Cider Vinegar** – typically made from apples and slightly sweet in taste. Cider vinegar is a fabulous start for great salad dressings.

**Fruit Vinegar** – white or wine vinegars that are infused with fruit or fruit juice and have a sweet and sour taste. Blueberry and raspberry are good choices.

**Herb Vinegar** – white or wine vinegars that are flavored by adding herbs, spices, or other seasonings. Basil, dill, garlic, and tarragon are popular additions. Herb vinegar is a nice addition to dressings.

**Malt Vinegar** – made from barley and very popular in England. Malt vinegar is often served with fish and chips.

**Rice Vinegar** – rice or rice-wine vinegar is made from fermented rice or rice wine. It is clear and has a very delicate and mild flavor. Rice vinegar is used in Asian recipes, salad dressings, and is good splashed on fruits and vegetables.

**Wine Vinegar** – made from red and white wines. Wine vinegars have smooth flavors and are great in marinades and salad dressings.

## OTHER VINEGAR USES IN THE KITCHEN:

❋For vegetables that are a little wilted, soak them in cold water and vinegar to perk them up.

❋Add a teaspoon of herb vinegar to a can of soup or a sauce to add some flavor and freshness.

❋For hands that have been stained by fruit or berries, wash them with vinegar, and bye-bye stains!

❋For icky smells in the kitchen, mix ½-part water and ½-part vinegar and simmer on the stove to eliminate them.

## UTILIZE YOUR MICROWAVE.

Moms will tell you that microwaves can be a huge help in the kitchen. (Most of us remember when they were invented!) Not only can they reheat leftovers and zap a bag of popcorn in a jiffy, they also perform many functions that speed up preparation and cooking time. Microwaves are great for defrosting frozen foods, melting butter or margarine (cover to avoid splatters!), and even boiling water. Although they are capable of doing a lot of *real* cooking, microwaves mostly come in handy for the little things. They are perfect for a few quick jobs when you don't have the time to use the stove.

**MOM-*sense*:** Frozen meats are better off being defrosted in the refrigerator for a couple of days. If you must use the microwave for defrosting, use the low setting and do it slowly.

### Time-Saving Microwavable Foods

**Bacon** – Line a plate with paper towels. Place bacon on plate, covering with another paper towel. Cooking on High, allowing about 1 minute per slice.

**Butter** – *To melt,* place butter or margarine in a bowl and heat on High for 40 seconds for 2 T., 45-60 seconds for ¼ cup, and 1 to 1 ½ minutes for ½ cup.

**Butter** – *To soften slightly,* heat ½ cup on Low for 1 to 2 minutes.

**Chocolate** – *To melt,* place chocolate in a bowl and heat on High 1-2 minutes per ounce. Stir after each minute.

**Cream cheese** – *To soften,* place cream cheese in a bowl and heat on Medium for 15-30 seconds for 3 ounces.

**Hot Fudge and other ice cream toppings** – Heat chilled toppings uncovered on High for 30 seconds to 1 ½ minutes for every ½ cup.

**Ice Cream** – *To soften,* heat frozen ice cream uncovered on High for 15 seconds per pint, or until soft.

**Potatoes** – *To bake,* prick the potato a couple of times with a fork and cook on High 4-6 minutes for 1 potato, 6-9 minutes for 2 potatoes, and 10-15 minutes for 4 potatoes. Let the potatoes rest for a few minutes before eating.

**MOM-*sense*:** For just-right potatoes, try putting them in a plastic grocery bag, tying a loose knot, then microwaving them. This seals in the moisture and makes them come out perfect!

**Tortillas** – *To warm and soften*, place a few tortillas between wet paper towels on a plate. Heat on High for 20-30 seconds.

**Vegetables** – *To steam,* place fresh, washed vegetables in a shallow, microwave-safe baking dish. Put only a few spoonfuls of water in with the vegetables. Cover with plastic wrap and cook for 4-5 minutes. Check for doneness, season to suit your taste, and enjoy.

## ENJOY GRILLING AND/OR BARBEQUING.

*Grilling* by definition is simply cooking food over a fire until it is done or cooked to your satisfaction. *Barbequing* is also cooking food over a fire, but it is done more slowly and usually the grill is covered with a lid. You don't need a master's degree to be able to grill or barbeque food (and contrary to popular belief, you don't have to be a male!), but you should know from the beginning that you might possibly make a few mistakes, burn a piece of meat, or drop one into the fire. Grilling really isn't all that difficult, but it does help to be prepared.

In the past, grilling was all about cooking a good piece of meat and enjoying the process. Today we have learned that you can grill just about anything. Why, just the other day I watched a cooking show and saw a guy grilling peaches! Fish, chicken, pizza, vegetables, and fruits are all finding their way onto a hot grill grid somewhere near you. It's exciting! You may as well jump on in and try your hand at it, too.

## Types of grills

**Charcoal** – Use charcoal briquettes that you buy at the grocery store. Be sure to bank them three- or four-high on one side of the grill for high heat and place a single layer on the other side for lower heat. By varying the heat strength, you can have control over your cooking. After you light your charcoal, let it burn down for several minutes before you begin cooking your food. *Don't cook your food over high flames*.

**Gas** – Most likely you will have a propane gas grill. The other type of gas grill includes a natural gas line

**Chicken** – Pierce with a fork or tongs. If juices run clear, then you can count on it being well done. If juices are not clear, then for heaven's sake, cook that chicken longer.

**Burgers** – Press in the center with your finger or with tongs. If juice flows freely, your burger is rare to medium rare. If some juice flows out, your burger is probably medium toward medium well. If no juice flows, your burger is well done.

**Steak and Chops** – Press with your finger or the backside of your tongs. If your steak feels soft, it is rare. If your steak feels firmer and is a little resistant to the touch, it is medium. If the steak is hard and doesn't give in to the touch, then it is well done. You can also judge steaks by their inside color: red is rare; pink is medium, and brown is well done.

**Fish** – Put aluminum foil on your grill and place fish on top of the foil or in a grill basket, and brush with oil or butter to help it not stick. Fish is done when it flakes easily with a fork and is opaque all the way through.

that hooks directly into your grill. If you are cooking with propane gas, make sure your tank is full before you begin. Turn your burners on high and light, then turn down to medium for cooking. *Don't forget to turn the gas off when you finish cooking.*

## MARINADES AND RUBS:

Flavor enhancers are great to use when grilling. It is fun to experiment with different flavors and to try new ways to prepare your grilled meats and veggies.

**Marinades** are liquids that are composed of flavor-enhancing ingredients. Combinations of vinegars, herbs, spices, citrus fruit juice, wines, beer, soy sauces, and oil will give foods new life when used before and during the grilling process. Meats can be marinated for up to six hours or even overnight to increase the flavor. It is fine to baste your meats, except chicken, with your marinade while they are cooking.

✛ Start with a clean grill surface. Scrub all the gritty leftovers from your last cook. Next, wipe the grate with a paper towel that you have doused with olive or vegetable oil.

✛ Never place your cooked, grilled food on the same plate that raw meat was on before cooking. Have a clean plate on hand, or wash the one previously used.

✛ A great way to have a side dish for your grilled meat is to grill some vegetables along with it. You won't have any messy pans or dishes to clean, and you'll be eating healthy as well.

✛ Grill chicken with the skin on. The flavor will be better, and the chicken won't burn as easily. You can always remove the skin when you eat the chicken. **Remember that sometimes it helps to parboil chicken— especially bone-in chicken —before grilling.**

✛ Warm your sauces before you baste your grilling meat because a cold sauce can slow down your cooking time.

✛ Let a steak sit or rest for a few Moments after removing from the grill. It will rise a few more degrees in temperature and allow the cooking process to slowly finish.

✛ **Never** use a marinade that raw chicken has been sitting in. Discard it and have another batch of marinade ready to baste with.

✛ Don't turn your meat until it is a bit crusty or seared. It will help to seal in the juices if it crusts on both sides.

✛ Buy a new paintbrush, about 1 to 1 ½ inches wide, to baste your food on the grill. These work better and last longer than basting brushes.

✛ Make sure that meat like steaks or chops are at room temperature before cooking. This will assure you of a quicker cooking time. **(This does not apply to chicken.)**

✛ When grilling shish kebobs, it is a great idea to place your meats on one skewer and your veggies on a separate one. Because it takes longer to cook the meat, your veggies won't be burned up; instead they will be perfectly cooked as well.

✛ Get creative when grilling your vegetables. Use some of those herbs and spices you bought along with oils or butter and maybe a few onions; then seal in foil for great flavor!

✛ Have a clean spray bottle full of water handy in case of flame-ups. If this happens, squirt 'em down.

If you enjoy the flavor of your marinade and want to use it at the table, prepare an extra recipe to use. You never want to use the same marinade that you had raw meat sitting in.

**MOM-*sense*:** For easy marinating, use a zipper-top plastic bag. It is perfect for turning the meat or vegetables without getting your hands dirty. Plus, clean-up is a breeze—just throw the bag in the garbage!

**Rubs** are mixtures of salt, pepper, spices, and herbs that are rubbed onto meat prior to grilling. The flavors of the dry rub mixture will penetrate the meat and enhance the flavor.

............................

## Veggies Good for Grilling:

Asparagus, corn-on-the-cob, eggplant, mushrooms, onions, peppers, potatoes, yellow squash, zucchini squash, and tomatoes are all delicious and tender when cooked on a grill. Be careful to use tongs when turning them. You can wrap them in foil or purchase inexpensive grilling pans to cook your veggies in. These pans are wonderful and allow you to cut your veggies into smaller pieces to combine with others.

............................

## REMEMBER THE GREEN STUFF!

Okay, I have to say it. No section on cooking and eating would be complete without this gentle reminder—no doubt, you've heard it before: *Eat your vegetables!* You know you should. A diet of carry-out pizza and Pringles just doesn't cut it.

**MOM-*sense*:** Did you know that many fruits and vegetables contain antioxidants, which help prevent diseases like cancer, stroke, and heart disease, and keep us healthy? Load up on tomatoes, blueberries, cherries, corn, carrots, mangos, grapes, and blackberries.

But keep in mind it's not just vegetables that you should be eating. You should also have some protein, carbohydrates, fats (yes, fats), and water to make sure you are getting enough vitamins and minerals. Eating right is essential to taking good care of your body. Well-balanced meals give you energy, prevent you from getting sick, and help your mind and body stay strong.

Eating well should be "good common sense." However, as you know, we don't always demonstrate common sense. For those of us who need a little nudge in the right direction, the U.S. Department of Agriculture recommends these dietary guidelines for healthy living:

1. Balance the food you eat with physical activity to maintain or improve your weight.
2. Choose a diet with plenty of grain products, vegetables, and fruits. (*Whole grains are best.*)
3. Choose a diet low in fat, saturated fat, and cholesterol.
4. Eat a variety of foods.
5. Choose a diet that is moderate in salt and sodium.
6. Choose a diet that is moderate in sugars.
7. If you drink alcoholic beverages, do so in moderation. (*Amen from Mom on this one!*)

Being healthy is not just for dieticians, world class athletes, and eccentric people who love tofu and yoga; it's for you, too! *You can* eat and feel healthy. You just need to commit to it—and take the time to make wise choices (and salads) rather than going the easy (or drive-thru) route. Go ahead! Mom thinks you're worth it, and your body will thank you for your efforts.

## JUST WHAT AND HOW MUCH YOU SHOULD EAT EVERY DAY

**Bread, cereal, rice, and pasta:** *6-11 servings*
Serving size: 1 slice bread, 1 dinner roll, ½ c. cooked rice, ½ hot dog or hamburger bun, 1 oz. (¼ c.) ready-to-eat cereal

**Milk, yogurt, and cheese:** *2-3 servings*
Serving size: 1 c. milk or yogurt, 1½ oz. natural cheese, 2 oz. processed cheese, about ¼ c.

**Vegetables:** *3-5 servings*
Serving size: ½ c. cooked or raw chopped vegetables, ¾ c. vegetable juice, 1 c. mixed green salad, ½ c. tomato or spaghetti sauce (no meat)

**Fruits:** *2-4 servings*
Serving size: 1 medium-sized apple, banana, orange, pear, or peach; ½ c. dried fruit, ½ c. canned, cooked, or frozen fruit, ¾ c. 100% fruit juice

**Meat, fish, poultry, beans, eggs, and nuts:** *2-3 servings*
Serving size: 2-3 oz. cooked lean meat, poultry, or fish; ⅓ c. nuts, ½ c. cooked dried beans, 2-3 equivalents of 1 oz. of meat; for example, 2 T. peanut butter or 1 egg = 1 oz. of meat

**Fats, oils, and sweets:** Eat as little as possible.

## KEEP IT REGULAR!
## ADD SOME FIBER TO YOUR DIET.

* Buy whole grain breads.

* Reach for the popcorn, not chips.

* Try eating brown rice instead of white.

* Add some fruit to your cereal.

* Don't peel your apple; eat the peeling, too.

* Try a bran muffin instead of your regular choice.

* Eat more fresh, raw vegetables.

* Try nuts and dried fruits instead of candy for a snack.

* Drink at least six glasses of water a day.

Read the labels that contain nutrition facts when you buy your food. Look for foods that are low in fats, sugars, sodium, and carbohydrates. The bottom line is to eat balanced meals. Your body needs a little something from each of the food categories. Remember that moderation is the key.

## SIMPLE WAYS TO CUT FAT

* Use more olive oil.

* Drink low-fat milk and milk products.

* Use 2% cheese.

* Add more fish to your diet.

* If you must fry foods, use peanut or canola oil.

* Avoid food high in saturated fat.

# J.A.M. Session: A little Q and A with MOM

## How do I avoid harmful bacteria in my kitchen?

Three simple words, my dear: **Wash your hands!** Prevent the spread of bacteria in your kitchen by washing your hands with soap often. Make an extra effort to wash your hands after handling raw meats, and go ahead and splurge on a squirt bottle of antibacterial spray for your kitchen countertops. It will be well worth the money spent to keep your kitchen clean and safe.

## My fruit keeps getting too ripe before I eat it. What should I do?

Don't be the Bearer of Bad Fruit—just freeze it! The best fruits to freeze are bananas, berries, grapes, melon, and peaches. Place your fruit in a single layer on a cookie sheet and slide into the freezer. Once it is frozen, put the fruit into plastic freezer bags. Take it out when you need it, let it thaw (or eat it frozen—yummy!), and tah dah, you have great fruit! You can keep it for up to one year in the freezer. For bananas, peel first and wrap each one in wax paper before placing in the bag. For peaches, peel first, slice, and remove the pit.

## How do I make a smoothie?

Got extra frozen fruit bagged up in the freezer? Toss it into the blender with some juice and a scoop of yogurt or ice cream for a delicious and quick smoothie. It's a great snack and pick-me-up!

## How do I keep my refrigerator's meat and veggie drawers clean?

Place paper towels in those drawers. This eliminates messes, especially if things leak or go bad!

## How long will my herbs and spices last?

The shelf life for most dried herbs is about one year. Check them for freshness at least one time a year. If you smell no aroma after you crush it, toss it out and replace it.

## Oh my gosh, my skillet is on fire! What do I do?

**Don't** douse it with water. Reach into the cupboard and grab either salt or baking soda and pour it on the flames.

## How do I get rid of smoke and strong food smells in the kitchen?

Open a window, turn on your stove fan, and light an aromatic candle to absorb the smells.

## How do I keep my oven clean?

Place aluminum foil on the bottom of the oven underneath the coils. When something spills over, simply replace the foil, and no harm done.

## Yuck! My soup has a greasy residue on the top of it!

Don't worry, just place a large leaf of lettuce in the soup to absorb the grease.

## How do I keep my cutting board clean?

Always wash it with hot, soapy water or run it through the dishwasher, especially if you have had raw meat on it.

## Should I throw away a pan that is scorched?

Heaven's no. Combine water and baking soda into a pasty mixture and cover the burned area. Give this time to rest for a couple of hours, and then it should be easier to remove.

## Oops! I just added way too much salt to a pot of soup or vegetables!

Never fear—simply peel a potato and drop it in the pot. The potato will absorb the salt. Discard it later. (I have had to drop in two or three potatoes before when I got a little carried away with the salt!)

## Got any tips on grating cheese?

Of course. Place the cheese in the freezer for half an hour and it will be much easier to grate than when it is soft.

## What about leftovers?

Get these goodies in the refrigerator within thirty minutes. Make sure they are covered tightly with plastic wrap, in a plastic zipper-top bag, or in a plastic container with a tight lid.

# Just one more thing . . .

✓ **Lay off the extra salt!** Too much salt in your diet can make your blood pressure go up, and you're too young for that.

✓ **Always simmer soups**, don't boil them.

✓ **Avoid tough crust.** If you don't want your baking bread to have a hard crust, place an ovenproof pan containing water on the lower oven shelf during the baking time.

✓ **Remember the ice cream!** Always keep a container of vanilla ice cream in your freezer. It goes with everything!

✓ **Go on nose patrol.** If something smells bad in your refrigerator, throw it out.

✓ **Don't mess up your hands when greasing a pan**. If a recipe demands that you use shortening to "grease a pan," don't get your hands messy. Use a paper towel to grab some shortening and spread it the same way. When you finish, your pan will be ready, and your hands will be clean.

✓ **Don't spray non-stick spray toward the floor when spraying a baking pan.** *If you miss,* your floor will be very slick.

✓ **BE A REBEL: Avoid fast-food restaurants.** The food is full of calories, salt, sugar, and fat—all the things that are bad for you. Plus, it gets expensive. If you really don't have a choice, make a good selection and go easy on the fries!

· · · · · · · · · · · · · · · · · · · · · · · · · · · · · · · · · · · · · · · · · · · · · · · · ·

## How to separate an egg:

❖ Crack the side of the egg on a flat surface.

❖ Over a bowl, use your thumbs to pull the shell apart.

❖ Divide the two parts of the egg by pouring the yolk back and forth between the eggshell cups and letting the egg white fall off into the bowl.

**MOM-*sense*:** If this sounds too intimidating, you can buy an inexpensive egg-separating tool.

## How to brew a good pot of coffee:

◆Choose a good, high-quality coffee.

◆Make sure the coffee is fresh.

◆Be sure the grind of the coffee matches your coffee maker.

◆Use a filter that fits your coffee maker.

◆Use 2 tablespoons of coffee for every 6 ounces of water.

◆Use clean, cold water in your coffee maker.

◆Turn on the coffee maker, and smell the aroma of the brewing coffee.

Pour yourself a cup and enjoy!

## How to "core" a head of iceberg lettuce:

∗Firmly grasp a head of iceberg on the opposite side of the core.

∗Hit the core against a cutting board or countertop.

∗The core should pull out easily.

∗Wash the lettuce under cold running water through the core.

∗Invert the head of lettuce to drain.

∗Store clean lettuce in a plastic zippered bag in the crisper drawer of your refrigerator. (Mom likes to soak iceberg in a bowl of cold water with 1 T. salt mixed in, then wash, drain, and store.)

# CHAPTER FIVE

# You, too, Can Entertain!

*"The true essentials of a feast are only fun and feed."*
— OLIVER WENDELL HOLMES, SR.

Entertaining in your own home can be so much fun—okay, it can be a lot of work, too, but it doesn't have to be overly stressful. The great thing about entertaining is, it's all up to you! You can invite one person over or twenty. It can be formal or more relaxed—it all depends on the preferences of the chef, activities director, and decorator (in other words, you).

Start out small when you begin to entertain: invite a few friends over to watch a game, and have everyone bring snack foods. You don't need to prepare an elaborate meal to entertain. You can just be the one who pulls it all together: the people, the place, the food, and the reason for gathering. No matter whether it is a small or a large group, you will want to have your place looking good and to be as hospitable as possible.

**First things first: Plan ahead.**
Doing a little planning ahead of time will ensure that you can be relaxed while you are entertaining. Planning is essential to being a successful host or hostess. Even if you only write things on the back of a bookmark, at least you are thinking ahead. You may just ask a few people over after work or when you see them out somewhere. No matter how it happens, do a little planning, even if it is only in your head.

An event that has been planned in advance flows so much better. True, sometimes spur-of-the-moment parties are great. But when you decide to go to a little more trouble and do something a little more special, you should make plans.

### PLANNING FOR A PARTY OR A MEAL:

✓ Establish why you are entertaining: sports event, friend's birthday, holiday, or celebratory dinner.

✓ Decide what type of entertaining you will do: cookout, intimate dinner, or potluck.

✓ Invite your guests: by invitation, e-vite, phone, or in person.

✓ Plan on where you will serve and how you will accommodate your guests: you might need to borrow chairs from a neighbor, for example.

✓ Plan your menu – do it all yourself, or ask for help from friends or family.

✓ Make lists of things you will need: food, drinks, ice, decorations, etc.

# Gather your serving essentials.

The first thing you need to do before you entertain is make sure you have at least a minimum of basic kitchenware for serving food and drinks. You do not need expensive or fancy things, just enough for the number of people you are having. Heck, you can even have a potpourri of mix and match dishes. If you are creative with what you have, people will think you planned it that way.

**MOM-*sense*:** If you have no idea how to decorate, look at some magazines for ideas, search the Net, or ask that Martha Stewart-like friend of yours. You don't have to copy their fancy ideas to a tee; just use them as a starting point. A local Party Store is another good place for ideas.

### SERVING ITEMS CHECKLIST

**Place settings** – *for four, six, or eight of dinner plates, salad plates, and bowls* (Some come in pre-packaged sets, which can be less expensive.)

**Flatware** – *forks, spoons, knives*

**Serving pieces** – *salad fork and spoon, serving spoons, big fork*

**Drinking glasses** – *Eight is a good start.* (And, of course, you must have a collection of plastic cups from every place you visit.)

**Mugs** – *for coffee, tea, and hot chocolate.* Raid your Mom's cabinet and come away with an eclectic collection of mugs.

**Wine glasses** – *Four to eight is a good number to have.*

**Serving bowls, platter** – *A couple of serving bowls, a platter for meat, and a salad bowl are a good starting point.*

**Paper plates, napkins, plastic cutlery, plastic or paper cups** – *Sometimes you just want to use them for easy clean-ups or because your meal is very casual.*

### SET THAT TABLE.

Having a table that is set properly is civilized, proper, inviting, and a little more formal. If you set the table before your guests arrive, it shows that you have put time and effort into your planning. It also gives them a hint how the night should unfold.

Your table should look nice, but it doesn't need to cost a fortune. You don't need sterling silver flatware and bone china to set a pretty table. Do your best at creating a good look, and don't worry about impressing your guests. If you are happy with the way it looks, then you can relax. Remember, your attitude sets the tone for the night.

**Checklist for a properly set Table:**
* Dinner plates
* Flatware: knife, fork, and spoon are essential; salad forks are optional
* General rule: knives and spoons on the right, forks on the left
* Place your plates and flatware one inch from the edge of your table
* Napkins: paper are fine, but cloth are nicer; make sure to fold them and place them in the center of the dinner plate or to the left of the fork
* Glasses: always include a water glass and another for wine, tea, or other beverages
* Salt and pepper shakers
* A centerpiece of some sort: never too tall to see through or around

**Proper Table Setting**

## REALIZE THAT BUFFETS ARE NOT JUST FOR CHINESE RESTAURANTS!

While setting a great looking table is the more formal and intimate way to go, meals in today's world can be a little more casual. More and more entertaining is done in a buffet-type service, where you set all the food out and allow people to serve themselves. Buffet serving is perfectly acceptable and much easier on the host or hostess. It also allows your guests to become involved in the serving process, while taking the pressure off of you.

### Buffet Serving Line Checklist

★Plates should always be at the beginning.

★Place your food together according to types: salads, veggies, meat, desserts.

★Have separate smaller plates for desserts.

★Have the flatware rolled up in a napkin to make sure your guests get each piece.

★Drinks should be at the end of the serving line so guests won't have to juggle while serving.

★If you are using paper plates, have your garbage can empty, accessible, and ready for clean-up.

## BE A GOOD HOST/HOSTESS.

You may feel a bit nervous at your first big (or little) dinner party, so take some advice from a well-practiced host: Mom. On the day or night of your special occasion, make sure that you have everything ready ahead of time so that when your guests arrive, you can focus on them and not on cooking or setting a table.

If you have dishes that must be cooked and assembled the day of the party, or other last minute actions, write out a detailed and timed schedule of what you will do the day of the party, so you will know exactly what to do and when. Beginning with a time about three or four hours before the guests are to arrive, write down each thing you need to do, and the time you will do it. (For example: 4:00, go pick up the flowers; 5:30, put the baked potatoes in the oven; 6:45, light the candles, etc.) This way you can make sure you have enough time for everything you've planned, and if you get in a tizzy, your list can guide you. Take a shower and relax while you are getting dressed. Turn on some music and set the mood or tone for the rest of the time. You should be the one to open the door as your guests ring the bell. (And it's best if you aren't holding a potholder with flour on your nose!)

MOM-*sense*: Be sure to take your guests' coats if it's cold outside.

One thing you need to remember is to not get stressed out about your event. If you made your plans and followed them, then you have nothing to worry about. Take a deep breath and relax. Your guests will feel it if you are uncomfortable. Put a smile on your face and enjoy yourself. After all, nobody enjoys or remembers dull parties, so make yours fun!

**MOM-*sense*:** Make sure your dishwasher is empty when your party begins so that you can load it when the party ends. (It's an even better idea to wash your prep utensils as you go to keep things clean and tidy.)

## Key points to remember when entertaining:

✛Invite people that have things in common with each other.

✛Make sure all your guests feel welcome, not just the people you know the best.

✛Watch out for guests who find themselves all alone.

✛Introduce new arrivals to others.

✛Bring up subjects or topics to keep the conversation from going flat.

✛Don't ever be overdressed; look nice, but be comfortable.

## BE A GOOD NEIGHBOR, TOO.

There will be times when you will not have enough of something you need to entertain. You may be short on plates, flatware, or even chairs to sit on. It is perfectly acceptable to borrow from a friend. I'm sure your own Mom raised you to have relationships with people that allow you to share what you have and help each other out. If so, remember to always return things in the same or better shape than when you got them. Always wash anything you borrow and make sure you return it clean. And, for heaven's sake return it a.s.a.p.—whether it's a tablecloth or a movie. Do not hang on to things that don't belong to you. You will get a bad reputation, and then no more borrowing for you.

Mom also wants you to understand and keep the #1 rule when you entertain: Remember your neighbors, and keep the noise level down at your get-togethers. No one wants to answer the door or phone to be berated by angry neighbors or to greet the police who have been called to ask you to be quiet. Just be aware of the noise and/or music and keep it to a minimum. Your reputation is irreplaceable, and heaven forbid that a grumpy neighbor might ask, "Don't they know better than to be playing loud music at 3 in the morning?! What kind of Mother raised them?"

## CONSIDER HAVING A THEME FOR YOUR GATHERING.

One of the best things you can do for yourself is to have a theme for your event. Themes make it easier on you, allowing you to be creative and add little touches that can be fun and special. Think of a theme for your party or meal, and ask a friend to help you get it all together. You'll have twice the fun!

Here are some possible ideas for a theme party. But don't let me limit your imagination . . .

## South of the Border/ Mexican Fiesta

Buffet style is best here, perhaps even on a porch/patio or out in the yard.

Use an inexpensive Piñata as a centerpiece and paper flowers as accents.

Don't try to be too fancy; colorful paper plates, napkins, and plastic cutlery work well for this feast.

Try a Mexican blanket as a tablecloth.

Have bowls of chips, salsa, and guacamole sitting around to munch on.

Have pitchers of margaritas or punch ready with colorful plastic cups waiting to be filled.

Fill a tub of ice with beer and soft drinks.

Create a taco or burrito bar by placing all the fixings in separate bowls lined up in the order for stuffing the tortillas and shells.

Ground beef, chicken, shredded jack cheese, shredded lettuce, chopped tomatoes, and sour cream are the usual fillings for burritos and tacos. (You can also do a "taco salad" type meal, where everyone adds whatever toppings they wish.)

Bowls of rice and beans should be ready, covered in plastic wrap and heated in the microwave just before serving.

Some great festive music will enhance your theme and give a nice backdrop.

## Brunch

*Serve between 10 a.m. and 1 p.m.*

❖ This is great for visiting parents or anyone from out of town.

❖ Prepare a set table or serve buffet style, depending upon the number of guests.

❖ Pottery or china is a nice touch for brunch, with colored cloth or paper napkins.

❖ A pitcher of Mimosas or Bloody Mary's will appeal to adults, along with juice, milk, water, and coffee.

❖ A blooming potted plant can work well as a centerpiece, or fresh flowers in a vase. Or try an arrangement of fresh fruits.

❖ Choices should include: eggs or an egg dish, bacon or sausage, grits, biscuits or a breakfast sweet bread, and a bowl of fresh fruit.

❖ Your table should include butter, jelly or jam, salt, and pepper.

## Game or Card Night

✓ Set up the playing table for cards or games.

✓ Food should be served on the kitchen counter.

✓ Prepare sandwiches cut into halves or quarters for easy eating.

✓ Set out 1 or 2 large bowls of chips.

✓ A hot or cold dip with crackers goes well on the side.

✓ A bucket on the counter with iced drinks is great for self service.

✓ A pot of coffee or hot tea after dinner keeps the action going.

✓ Brownies or cookies make an easy pick-up dessert.

✓ You can always have bowls of nuts or trail mix on the game tables.

✓ If you're keeping score, it's fun to have a small gift for the person with the highest score—and the lowest!

## Movie Night

∗ Select a movie ahead of time and prepare a meal that complements the movie; for instance, select *The Godfather* and have an Italian meal.

∗ Prepare spaghetti and meatballs (or whatever food matches your movie theme).

∗ Toss a quick Caesar salad.

∗ Warm a loaf of French bread.

∗ Open a bottle of red wine, and serve iced water.

∗ Serve tiramisu or cannolis for dessert (pick some up on the way home!).

## Potluck

✛ A quilt makes a beautiful and unique tablecloth.

✛ Place all dishes in a buffet-style serving line.

✛ Select a main dish and prepare that yourself.

✛ Ask someone to bring a salad.

✛ Ask someone to bring a vegetable.

✛ Ask someone to bring bread.

✛ Ask someone to bring dessert.

✛ Have beverages ready when your guests arrive.

✛ Compliment your guests on the food they contributed.

## Barbecue/Cookout

∗ A tube of sunscreen on the table may come in handy (and depending on where you live, a can of bug repellant).

∗ Inexpensive paper tablecloths are great and make clean-up a breeze.

∗ Paper plates, napkins, and plastic cutlery are a must.

∗ Burgers, hot dogs, and chicken are easy to grill and usually are a hit. Having choices is nice.

∗ Prepare a plate or bowls ahead of time with sliced tomatoes, sliced and chopped onions, shredded lettuce, and pickles. A cold salad (potato, cole slaw, or ramen noodle) is nice, but not necessary.

∗ Have baked beans warming in the oven and corn on the cob wrapped in foil staying warm, too.

∗ Tubs full of iced drinks in individual sizes make it easy for everyone to help themselves.

*Cold pitchers of lemonade are delicious when served over ice in colored plastic cups.

*Use condiments in squeeze bottles for easy use: ketchup, mustard, mayonnaise, and relish.

*Dessert can be as simple as buying a watermelon and cutting it into small wedges or as nostalgic as making a freezer of homemade ice cream.

*For s'mores fixings: fill a plate with graham crackers, marshmallows, Hershey's chocolate bars, and have bamboo skewers available to bring back fun memories of childhood.

## Holidays

◆Decorate depending upon the season: Easter Eggs in the Spring, Flags and Flowers in the Summer; Pumpkins, Mums, and Gourds in the Fall; Lights, Christmas Balls, and Poinsettias in the Winter.

◆Include dear family and friends on your list.

◆Make or ask others to prepare everyone's favorite dishes.

◆Hug and reminisce.

◆Take lots of photos. As a possible "party favor," give each family a small photo book, and then send everyone pictures of the party once they're developed.

◆Eat until you can't eat anymore.

◆Eat leftovers until you can't take it anymore or the food is all gone.

◆Look forward to doing it all again next year.

## Tailgating at the Stadium or at Home

*Dress in appropriate team colors.

*Use pom-pom shakers in your team's colors for your centerpiece.

*Try using a team blanket as a tablecloth.

*Encourage your friends to paint their faces, or have temporary tattoos available.

*Mix and match paper plates, cups, napkins, and plastic cutlery in team colors.

*Finger foods of all kinds are welcome at this party: chicken wings, sandwiches, chili, bratwurst, hot dogs, chips, veggies, hot and cold dips, etc.

*Baskets are great to use for serving your food.

*A packed cooler of drinks is a must.

*Have a CD of upbeat music playing.

*Don't forget to yell for your team!

## Picnics

*Pack a large basket with paper plates, napkins, and plastic cutlery.

*Pull out your favorite blanket or quilt to sit on.

*Prepare or buy your favorite picnic foods like fried chicken, pimento cheese sandwiches, PB&J sandwiches, tuna or chicken salad sandwiches, potato salad, deviled eggs, chips, pickles, cold soft drinks, lemonade, brownies, and cookies.

*Find a large shade tree, perhaps

near a cool running stream.

★Spread your blanket and enjoy your picnic meal with someone special.

## Dinner Party

❀Keep the number of guests small, between four and eight.

❀Set your table with plates, silverware, napkins, and glasses.

❀Buy fresh flowers and place in a vase, and use a couple of candles on the table.

❀Have pleasant music playing in the background.

❀Settle on a menu that is not extremely difficult and one that has recipes that can be prepared in advance.

❀Have at least four courses in your meal: soup, salad, entrée, and dessert.

❀Serve wine or tea and water.

❀Dessert can be served in another room with coffee.

❀Keep conversation lively and moving.

## Birthdays

✿It is preferable to have a birthday celebration be a surprise, because everyone loves to be remembered on their birthday, even if they say they don't.

✿Invite only those closest to the birthday boy or girl.

✿Buy balloons for the birthday honoree, no matter how old they are.

✿Be sure to have a birthday cake or cupcakes; candles are required!

✿Have a pack of matches or a lighter for the candles.

✿Ice cream is also required, with a scoop!

✿Plates and forks/spoons need to be stacked and ready to use.

✿Be sure to have a knife for the cake.

✿"Happy Birthday" is best sung really loud!

✿Take lots of photos for the Momentous occasion.

## Is it okay for me to use paper plates when I have people over?

Sure! Paper plates and other paper products are great for entertaining. Available in a wide variety of colors and themes, they assure you of easy and fast clean-ups so that you can spend more time with your guests. Also, using paper products keeps the get-together more casual and eases the comfort level of everyone.

## I'm having about eight people over. Do I need to send out invitations?

No, it's fine to call on the phone. Sometimes, that kind of invite is more personal anyway, and helps you know for sure who's coming.

## Is background music always necessary?

No, sometimes it can be distracting. If conversation is good, you don't need it. It's nice when people are coming in; just make sure it's not deafening!

# Just one more thing . . .

❖**Keep a camera sitting out each time you entertain.** Take photos yourself, or ask others to take a few. Regardless of who takes them, you will appreciate the tangible reminders of the fun you all had.

❖**Always make sure your bathrooms are clean before you entertain.** Your guests will use this room and will remember if it is clean or not. It's always considerate to have a candle or air freshener available in this room as well.

❖**Tired of ordering delivery pizza, but still crave it? Why not make your own?** Buy a pizza crust, use your own marinara or sauce from a jar, add shredded mozzarella cheese, and the toppings of your choice: pepperoni, sausage, mushroom, pepper, onion, artichokes, olives, chicken, pineapple, etc. You can even have individual crusts and have a pizza-making party!

*"At a dinner party, one should eat wisely, but not too well, and talk well, but not too wisely."*
— WILLIAM SOMERSET MAUGHAM

# CHAPTER SIX

# Life Beyond Ramen Noodles: Recipes to Impress!

*"One cannot think well, love well, sleep well, if one has not dined well."*

— **VIRGINIA WOOLF**

Mom realizes how tough it can be when you are learning to cook, so with that in mind, I now include some of the easiest and tastiest recipes on the planet. Each recipe listed here has only a few ingredients and takes very little time to prepare. Many of the ingredients will be found in your pantry or refrigerator.

Typically, these recipes will feed three to four people, unless otherwise stated. Usually, they will require ingredients you can find at any neighborhood grocery store. And most definitely, they will do what good food is supposed to do: fill the stomach, brighten the eyes, and gladden the heart!

## First things first:
## Keep it simple!

There is absolutely no reason to make cooking so difficult when you are just getting started. My hope is that you will try some of these and learn your way around your kitchen. You may even find a recipe for something your own Mom made you that you have been craving. Most of all, I really hope that you will come to enjoy cooking and that you will love to entertain and serve others. Nothing comforts quite like good food from a loved one. It is both satisfying and fun.

*Bon appétit.*

# Start with the starters.

You will see by the following heading that this category of fun foods has several names. And though the French may have given us the fancy word *hors d'oeuvres*, most Moms I know affectionately call them "finger foods" (maybe because it's easier to spell). You can serve these goodies as a prequel to a great meal, as snacks during a game or party, or even combine several of them to make a complete meal! You can't go wrong with these dips and snacks. As the Colonel used to say, they're finger-lickin' good!

## APPETIZERS
## HORS d'OEUVRES
## FINGER FOODS

### Hot Artichoke Dip

*2 cans artichoke hearts, drained*
  *& chopped*
*1 c. mayonnaise*
*1 c. finely grated Parmesan cheese*
*Pepper*
*Paprika*

Mix all ingredients and place in a small ovenproof dish that has been sprayed with nonstick cooking spray. Sprinkle extra Parmesan cheese generously on top and a little pepper and paprika. Bake at 350 degrees for 30-45 minutes or until very bubbly. *Serve hot with crackers, bagel chips, or French bread rounds.*

### Spinach Dip

*1 frozen package chopped spinach,*
  *thawed & drained on paper towels*
*1 c. mayonnaise*
*1 c. sour cream*
*1 package dry vegetable soup mix*
*1 can chopped water chestnuts*

Combine all ingredients and chill for a couple of hours. *Serve in a bowl surrounded by crackers, or scoop out a round bread loaf and serve with bread pieces.*

## Tasty Oyster Crackers

*½ c. vegetable or olive oil*
*2 T. dill weed*
*1 T. garlic salt*
*1 envelope Ranch dressing mix*
*1 box or bag of oyster crackers*

Sprinkle all ingredients over the oyster crackers in a large bowl. Stir very well. Place the coated crackers in a large plastic zippered bag. Give the bag a couple of good shakes every 30 minutes. Chill in the refrigerator for an hour or two. *Serve in a large bowl and watch them disappear.*

## Carla's Mexican Dip

*1-8 oz. pkg. cream cheese, softened*
*1-15 oz. can chili with beans*
*1-4.5 oz. can jar chopped green chilies*
*2 c. shredded cheese*

Begin by using an attractive plate or a very shallow baking dish (must be microwave safe). Spread cream cheese on the bottom as the first layer. Next, add the chili, green chilies, and cheese in the order listed. Microwave for 1 minute and check. Continue microwaving in 30-second intervals until the cheese has melted. *Serve with tortilla chips.*

## Simple Guacamole

*3 ripe avocados*
*2 T. salsa*
*1 t. minced garlic*
*Juice of ½ lime (fresh lime only)*
*¼ t. salt or garlic salt*

Seed and peel the avocados. Mash ripe avocados with a fork, but don't make too smooth. There should still be some avocado texture. Add all the other ingredients. *Serve with tortilla chips.*

**MOM-*sense*:** If your guacamole starts to darken in color, stir it around to perk up the color.

## 9 Layer Dip by Vickie

*1-14 oz. can refried beans*
*1 pkg. taco seasoning*
*1-16 oz. container guacamole*
*1-16 oz. sour cream*
*1 small jar of taco sauce*
*Shredded cheese*
*Shredded lettuce*
*1, 4.5 oz can chopped green chilies*
*Green onions, chopped*
*Cherry tomatoes, sliced in halves*

Mix ½ of the taco seasoning with the sour cream and the other ½ with the refried beans. Then, in a shallow dish, layer the ingredients exactly in the order given. Cover with plastic wrap and refrigerate until ready to serve. *Serve with tortilla chips.*

## Easy Salsa

1 - 28 oz. can whole peeled tomatoes
½ bunch fresh cilantro
1 t. minced garlic
1 small jalapeno pepper, diced fine;
    toss seeds if you don't like it too hot
Juice of 1 fresh lime

Chop tomatoes to your desired size.
Add all other ingredients and let sit
for at least ½ hour before serving.
*Serve with tortilla chips.*

**MOM-*sense*:** If you have a food
processor, put all ingredients in it
and blend the salsa together.

## Cindy's Reuben Dip

1-8 oz. pkg. cream cheese, softened
    & cut into bits
½ c. sour cream
2 t. onion, finely chopped
1 T. ketchup
2 T. spicy brown mustard
1 c. grated Swiss cheese
1 c. chopped sauerkraut,
drained
½ lb. corned beef, chopped

Combine cream cheese and
sour cream with mixer or in food
processor. Add next 3 ingredients.
Next, stir in the sauerkraut, Swiss
cheese, and corned beef. Place in
a small baking dish that has been
sprayed with nonstick cooking
spray. Bake covered with a lid or
aluminum foil at 375 degrees for 30
minutes. Remove the cover and bake
5 minutes longer. *Serve with rye
crackers or party bread.*

# Better make some beverages.

Down South where I'm from, no
meal is complete without a glass
of iced tea. And no self-respecting
Southern Mom serves tea without
lemons! Whether you're a tea drinker
or prefer a warmer (or stronger)
drink, the following recipes are
delightful ways to wet your whistle!

## DRINKS, BEVERAGES, AND BREWS

## Southern Sweet Iced Tea

4 tea bags (regular size)
2 c. water
1 c. sugar

Bring water to boil in a small
saucepan. Drop in tea bags, cover,
and remove from
heat. Let steep
for 5 minutes
(very important).
Meanwhile, place
sugar in a 2-quart
pitcher and dissolve
sugar with about 2 cups
of very hot water. Pour
warm tea into sugar
water mixture, holding
back tea bags. Cover tea
bags with hot water again and
pour into pitcher until it is full. *Serve
over ice with sliced lemons. To make
one gallon, add 4 more tea bags
and 1 more cup of sugar.*

## Summer Fruit Tea

*2 c. sugar*
*2 c. water*
*4 large tea bags or 8 small*
*2 c. orange juice*
*1 c. lemon juice*

Bring water and sugar to a rolling boil, add the tea bags, cover, and remove from heat. Let steep for 10 minutes. Pour juices into a one-gallon pitcher and add tea/water/sugar mixture, holding back tea bags. Cover tea bags with water again and pour into pitcher. Continue to fill with water until you have 1 gallon. *Serve over ice with a lemon slice or mint sprig.*

## Sangria

*1 lemon, sliced*
*1 or 2 oranges, sliced*
*½ c. sugar*
*Juice of 1 lemon*
*½ c. orange juice*
*1 quart Chianti wine*
*½ bottle (28 oz.) club soda*

Place lemon and orange slices in a pitcher. Add sugar and juices, and stir to dissolve sugar. Stir in wine. Refrigerate for several hours. Pour in club soda at the last minute before serving in ice-filled glasses. Serves 6-8 people.

## Fresh Fruit Smoothie

*1 quart orange juice*
*1 c. fresh strawberries*
*2 bananas*
*3 ice cubes*
*Fresh whole strawberries for garnish*

Combine half of the first 4 ingredients in a blender. Process until frothy. Pour into glasses and garnish with a whole fresh strawberry or a slice of a fresh strawberry. Repeat with the remaining ingredients. Makes 4 smoothies.

**MOM-*sense*:** Try making smoothies with other juices, like white grape or apple.

## Fresh Lemonade

*2 c. fresh lemon juice*
*3 c. sugar*
*Lemon slices*

Place the sugar and a cup of very hot water into a one-gallon pitcher and mix until the sugar dissolves. Stir in the lemon juice and add enough cold water to fill the pitcher. Stir until all ingredients are mixed well. *Serve over ice and place a slice of lemon on top of each glass to garnish.*

## Bloody Marys

1- 46 oz. can tomato juice or
   V8 juice
1 T. Worcestershire sauce
1 t. salt
1 t. pepper
2 T. lemon juice
1 c. vodka
Tabasco or your favorite hot sauce
Celery sticks

Into a one-gallon pitcher, pour
the tomato juice and add the
Worcestershire sauce, salt, pepper,
lemon juice, and vodka. Add about 4
shakes of the hot sauce into the mix,
unless you like more. Stir this very
well. *Serve over ice with a celery
stick for garnish.*

## Frozen Margaritas

¾ c. tequila
¼ c. triple sec orange liqueur
1 - 6 oz. can frozen limeade
Salt
Lime slices

In a blender, pour the tequila, triple
sec, and the limeade. Add enough
ice to fill your blender, and blend
the mixture well. Take a slice of lime
and rub it around the rim
of your glass, and then dip your
glass in salt. Fill your glass with a
frozen margarita. *Delicious with
Mexican foods.*

## Mimosas

Champagne
Orange Juice

Fill a wine glass or juice-sized glass
half full of orange juice. Then
add chilled champagne until full.
*Delicious when served with brunch.*

## Warm Apple Cider Tea

6 small tea bags (or 3 family-sized
   large bags)
8 c. water
3 cinnamon sticks
¾ c. sugar
1 lemon, thinly sliced
1-64 oz. jug or bottle of apple cider

In a large saucepan or pot, bring tea
bags, water, cinnamon sticks, and
lemon slices to the boiling point.
Reduce the heat and simmer for
about 20 minutes. Then, remove the
tea bags, cinnamon sticks, and lemon
slices. Add the sugar and stir well,
until the sugar has dissolved. Pour
in the apple cider and simmer again.
*Serve in mugs or cups.*

**MOM-*sense*:** This warm tea is great
on a cold day or at night sitting in
front of a fire or movie.

# Bring on the breakfast!

Moms (and nutritionists) everywhere call breakfast the most important meal of the day. Important or not, it certainly is one of the best! From a "simple" fried egg to a more complicated quiche or casserole, every cook needs to have a good armory of breakfast dishes to feed hungry troops now and then. (Even though these foods come under the "breakfast" heading, don't be afraid to cook them at other times. They can sure hit the spot on a cold winter's night!)

## BREAKFAST FOODS

### Eggs (Fried): "Sunny Side Up"

*(cooking the egg only on the bottom side)*
*2 eggs*
*1 T. butter*
*Salt*
*Pepper*

Melt butter in skillet over medium heat. Break one egg over a saucer or shallow bowl and gently slide it into the skillet. Cook the egg slowly so that the top of the egg is done before the bottom of the egg is overdone. The yolk will be very runny.

MOM-*sense*: Most people break the eggs directly over the skillet, but there is always the chance that shells could get into the pan.

### Eggs (Fried): "Over Easy"

*(cooking the egg on both sides once)*
Begin as in the *"sunny side up"* egg, but flip once when the bottom is set. The yolk will still be runny.

### Eggs (Fried): "Hard" or "Over-Well"

*(cooking the egg completely)*

Begin as *"sunny side up,"* but flip a couple of times to set the yolk. You can also break the yolk when you flip the egg so that the yolk is evenly cooked and spread over the white. The yolk should be completely cooked & firm.

### Eggs (Scrambled)

*4 eggs*
*2 T. milk*
*1 T. butter*
*Salt*
*Pepper*

Whisk eggs, milk, salt, and pepper until well blended. Melt butter in 8-inch skillet. Pour in egg mixture. Cook and do not stir until mixture starts to set on the bottom. Drag a spatula through the middle and continue until eggs are cooked and thicker, but still a little moist. Do not overcook or the eggs will be dry. Makes 2-3 servings.

## Eggs (Hard-Boiled)

*Eggs*
*Water*
*Ice*

Place the number of eggs you need in a saucepan. Cover the eggs with cool water until 1 inch above eggs. Place over high heat and bring just to boiling point. Boil for 10 minutes. Pour water off, cover with cold water, and add ice. As you are filling the pan with cold water, tap each egg against the pan to crack it. Let the eggs sit in ice water for 5 minutes. Crack and peel under slow-running cold water. *You may think this is too simple for a recipe, but I guarantee that countless Moms have received phone calls asking how to boil an egg!*

## Omelets

*3 eggs*
*1 T. butter*
*Salt*
*Pepper*
*Fillings of your choice*
   *Popular choices are: shredded cheese, chopped ham, onions, peppers, tomatoes, mushrooms, asparagus, (cooked) sausage and/or bacon*

Heat butter in a small skillet over medium-high heat. Whisk eggs with salt and pepper while pan is heating. Whisk well so that lots of air is incorporated into the eggs. This will ensure that you will have a light and fluffy omelet.

Pour eggs into the skillet and reduce the heat to medium. Continue to whisk the eggs while shaking the skillet, allowing the uncooked eggs to run past the cooked parts. Stop whisking when the eggs are evenly cooked. Push together holes in the eggs with a rubber spatula.

Place desired fillings on one side of the eggs. Run a spatula around entire edge of cooked eggs, then place it under the side without fillings and fold that side over the top of the fillings. Take the skillet and gently tip it toward a plate and let your omelet slide out. Enjoy.

**MOM-*sense*:** Always add cheese to an omelet last before the fold-over. It helps hold the omelet together. Omelets take a little practice, so if at first you don't succeed, fry, fry again!

## Quiche Lorraine

*1 refrigerated piecrust*
*1 med. onion, chopped*
*2 T. vegetable oil*
*6 slices bacon, cooked & crumbled*
*3 eggs, beaten*
*1 ½ c. milk*
*¼ t. salt*
*1 ½ c. Swiss cheese, grated*
*1 T. plain flour*

Sauté onion in large skillet in oil until onion is tender. Drain on paper towels. In large mixing bowl, combine eggs, milk, and salt. Stir in bacon and onion. In a separate bowl, mix Swiss cheese and flour. Next, add the cheese to the egg mixture and mix all ingredients well.

Pour the egg mixture into the pie shell that has been placed into a glass or metal pie pan. Bake at 325 degrees for 40 minutes or until a knife inserted into the center comes out clean. Let the quiche sit for 5-10 minutes before serving.

**MOM-***sense*: To keep your pie shell edges from becoming burned and hard, cover the edges with aluminum foil until the last ten minutes of baking.

## Granny's Waffles
*2 c. plain flour*
*3 t. baking powder*
*½ t. salt*
*2 T. sugar*
*2 eggs*
*¾ c. shortening*
*1 ½ c. milk*

Melt the shortening and allow it to cool. Beat eggs and add milk. Slowly add dry ingredients. Blend in shortening last. Pour into a heated waffle iron that has been sprayed with nonstick cooking spray. *Serve with butter or whipped cream and syrup.*

## Quick French Toast
*⅓ c. milk*
*1 t. vanilla extract*
*¼ t. salt*
*3 eggs, beaten*
*8 slices of bread*
*Powdered sugar*

Mix all first 5 ingredients in a mixing bowl. Pour into a shallow baking dish or pie plate. Dip the bread into the mixture and coat on each side. Sauté each slice of bread in melted butter until brown and crisp. Add butter as necessary. Shake powdered sugar over toast using a strainer. *Serve with syrup or fruit.*

**MOM-***sense*: Bread that is more than a day or two old is better to use than fresh. Also, you can use thicker bread like Texas Toast if you choose. If so, you might need to mix another recipe of batter.

## Simple Sausage & Egg Bake

*1 lb. sausage, fried, drained, and crumbled*
*6-8 eggs, beaten with milk, salt, & pepper*
*1 pkg. refrigerated crescent rolls*
*2 c. grated cheddar cheese*

Spray a 9 x 13 baking dish with nonstick cooking spray. Open crescent roll package and spread it on the bottom of the dish in one entire piece. Press the seams together. Sprinkle the sausage and cheese on top of dough. Pour egg mixture over it all. Bake at 375 degrees for 30-45 minutes. *This is a great dish to have for a brunch.*

## Garlic & Cheese Grits

*2 c. quick cook grits, cooked according to package*
*2 rolls garlic cheese (found by cheese in cold section of grocery store)*
*1 stick butter*
*½ c. milk*
*Salt & pepper to taste*
*Parmesan cheese*

Add butter and cheese to the cooked grits. Next add salt and pepper. Slowly stir in milk. Pour mixture into a suitably sized baking dish that has been sprayed with nonstick cooking spray. Sprinkle Parmesan cheese on top. Bake at 300 degrees for 30-40 minutes.

## Sour Cream Coffee Cake

*Batter:*
*8 oz. sour cream*
*2 eggs*
*½ c. butter, room temperature*
*1 c. sugar*
*2 c. plain flour*
*½ t. salt*
*1 t. baking soda*

*Filling:*
*1 t. cinnamon*
*½ c. sugar*
*½ c. finely chopped nuts, (pecans or walnuts work best)*

Mix batter together in one bowl, and filling in another. Using a round bundt or tube pan, spray with nonstick cooking spray and then layer the batter mixture on the bottom. Next, layer the filling on top. Using a table knife, cut into the mixture and go around the pan a couple of times. Bake at 325 degrees for 45 minutes.

**MOM-*sense*:** You can also bake this in an 8 x 8 or 9 x 9 square baking dish. Watch the baking time after 30 minutes.

## Banana Bread

*2 eggs*
*1 c. sugar*
*3 very ripe bananas, mashed*
*1 c. all purpose flour*
*½ c. butter, at room temperature*
*1/3 c. chopped pecans, optional*

Cream the eggs and sugar together. Add the remaining ingredients and beat well with an electric mixer. Pour into a loaf pan that has been sprayed with nonstick cooking spray. Bake for 45 minutes at 325 degrees.

## Fruit Dip

*3 T. sugar*
*1 egg, beaten*
*2 T. lemon juice*
*2 T. pineapple juice*
*½ c. whipped topping or*
*   whipped cream*

Mix together first 4 ingredients and cook over medium high heat until thick, stirring constantly. Remove from heat and cool. Stir whipped topping into the mix. Place in refrigerator until chilled completely. *Serve in a small bowl on a plate surrounded by fresh fruit. Fruits that work best are strawberries, blueberries, grapes, cantaloupe, pineapple, honeydew melon, and kiwi. (Also try other fresh fruits that are in season.)*

## SERVE SOME SAVORY SALADS.

Mom still remembers when iceberg was king. But those days have passed, and thanks to fun additions like Chinese noodles, toasted almonds, dried cranberries, and a rainbow of salad dressings, the days of boring salads are over! Try some of these variations for some tasty (and healthy) lunch or dinner fare.

MOM-*sense*: Use an egg slicer to make beautiful slices of fruits like strawberries, bananas, and kiwi for the tops of salads or to garnish your plate.

### SALADS

## Tuna Salad

*(every Mom's standby)*
*2 cans white albacore tuna,*
*   or tuna packed in water, drained*
*2 hard-boiled eggs, chopped*
*1/3 c. sweet pickle relish or chopped*
*   sweet pickles (more if you like)*
*½ c. mayonnaise*

Mix all ingredients together and chill. *Serve on bread with lettuce & tomato for a traditional sandwich.*

MOM-*sense*: Spread tuna salad on bread and add a slice of American or cheddar cheese and sauté in melted butter until toasted for a great Tuna Melt.

## Chicken Salad

*4 large chicken breasts, bone & skin on*
*1 c. celery, diced in small pieces*
*1 ½ c. mayonnaise*
*Salt*
*Pepper*
*Olive oil*

Wash chicken breasts, dry with paper towels and rub with olive oil, then sprinkle with pepper & salt. Place on a cookie sheet and roast in a 375 degree oven for 40 minutes or until cooked completely. Let the chicken cool, then peel skin off and pull chicken off the bone. Cut the chicken into small pieces and place in a large mixing bowl. Add the celery, and then stir in the mayonnaise. You may add more mayonnaise to achieve the consistency you prefer. Cover and refrigerate for 30 minutes prior to eating.

*Note: If you like your chicken salad with pickle, add ½ c. of diced sweet pickle.*

## Egg Salad

*6 hard-boiled eggs, chopped*
*2 T. sweet pickle relish*
*½ t. Dijon mustard*
*¼ c. mayonnaise*
*Dash of pepper*
*Dash of salt*

Place chopped eggs into mixing bowl. Add salt & pepper to eggs. Add other ingredients. Mix eggs, pickle relish, mustard, and mayonnaise. Cover and refrigerate 30 minutes before serving. *Note: Use yellow mustard if you prefer.*

## Mom's Potato Salad

*8 medium potatoes*
*¾ c. chopped celery*
*⅓ c. chopped onion*
*¾ c. chopped green pepper*
*½ c. chopped dill pickles*
*4 hard-boiled eggs, chopped*
*Salt*
*Pepper*
*1 ¼ c. mayonnaise*

Place potatoes and enough water to cover them in a large saucepan, and bring the water to a boil. Reduce the heat and simmer for 25 minutes. Drain the potatoes and allow them to cool. Peel the potatoes and cut them into cubes.

Place the potatoes in a large bowl and sprinkle generously with salt and pepper. Add the celery, onion, green pepper, pickles, and eggs. Stir in the mayonnaise until well mixed. Refrigerate until chilled, and serve.

## Cole Slaw

1 bag angel hair shredded
  cole slaw mix
1 medium onion, chopped
1 medium green pepper, chopped
Salt
Pepper
1 T. yellow mustard
½ c. mayonnaise

Rinse & drain cole slaw. Add
onion and pepper to slaw mix.
Sprinkle with salt and pepper. Add
mayonnaise and mustard. Mix very
well and refrigerate before eating.

## Aunt Gin's Best Green Salad

8 c. salad greens, (romaine
  works great)
2 cans mandarin oranges, drained
8 oz. chopped dates
1 red onion, sliced into rings

*Dressing:*
¼ c. salad oil
2 T. lemon juice
1 t. salt
¼ t. pepper
1 t. Worcestershire sauce

Add dressing when ready to serve
and toss well in a large mixing bowl.
*Goes well with most everything.*

## Caesar Salad

*(the fast & easy way)*
1 bag of Romaine lettuce,
  already in pieces
1 bottle of Caesar dressing mix
1 c. of Caesar croutons
Shredded Parmesan cheese

Toss in a large bowl and serve.
Sprinkle extra shredded Parmesan
cheese on top.

## Chef's Salad

1 head iceberg lettuce, cleaned and
  torn into bite-size pieces
1 tomato, cut into wedges
1 c. cooked ham, cut into thinly
  sliced strips
1 c. cooked chicken or turkey, cut
  into thinly sliced strips
1 c. cheddar cheese, cut into thinly
  sliced strips
2 hard-boiled eggs, cut into wedges
Salad dressing of your choice

Layer in the order listed, or toss
together randomly. *This salad is
traditionally served with Thousand
Island dressing, but feel free to
choose your own.*

## Cobb Salad

1 head iceberg lettuce, washed
  & drained
2 hard-boiled eggs, chopped
2 Roma tomatoes, sliced thinly
1 avocado, peeled & diced
1 chicken breast, skinned &
  boned, sliced
6 slices bacon, cooked & crumbled
Dressing of your choice

Cut iceberg lettuce into 4 wedges. Place each on a salad plate or in shallow bowls. Chop your lettuce or leave in wedges. Top lettuce with eggs, tomatoes, avocado, chicken & bacon. Drizzle with your favorite salad dressing.

## Braeburn Apple Salad

Bag of Spring Mix Salad
2 Braeburn apples, chopped
  and unpeeled
  (can substitute another apple)
Craisins, to taste
Chopped pecans, sautéed in butter
Blue cheese (optional)

### Dressing:
½ c. sugar
¼ c. apple cider vinegar
¼ c. Dijon mustard
¾ c. vegetable oil

Mix dressing until thick. To preserve apples, toss them in dressing, along with Craisins and pecans. Store mixture in refrigerator and toss with the lettuce right before serving.

## Crunchy Broccoli Salad

2 bunches broccoli, cut
  into flowerets
8 slices cooked bacon, crumbled
1 c. shredded cheddar cheese
1 red onion, sliced into rings

### Dressing
2 T. red wine vinegar
1 c. mayonnaise
⅓ c. sugar

Combine first 4 ingredients in a mixing bowl. Whisk the dressing ingredients together and toss over the salad. Can be refrigerated for a couple of days. Toss again before eating. *Note: ½ c. raisins and 1 c. sunflower seeds can be used in place of the bacon and cheese for a healthier salad.*

## Spinach Salad

1 bag fresh baby spinach, washed
  & dried
2 hard-boiled eggs
6 slices of cooked bacon, crumbled
1 red onion, sliced into rings
  & halved

### Dressing
1 c. oil, vegetable or olive
½ c. red wine vinegar
½ c. sugar
⅓ c. ketchup

Toss spinach, onion, bacon, eggs, and bacon in a large bowl. Pour in salad dressing a small amount at a time and toss until coated to your taste.

## Taco Salad

*1 lb. ground beef or turkey*
*1 pkg. taco seasoning mix*
*½ head iceberg lettuce, chopped*
*2 tomatoes, chopped*
*1 bag Fritos chips or small*
  *tortilla chips*
*Sour cream*
*Cheddar cheese, grated*

Brown beef or turkey, drain, and add taco mix according to directions on package. Layer half of chips, meat, lettuce, cheese, and tomatoes. Repeat layers. Serve and add a dollop of sour cream on each serving.

## SOOTHE (AND SATISFY) WITH SOUPS.

Some days, nothing soothes your inner hunger like a steaming bowl of soup. When you feel a bit nostalgic for home but don't have time to get there, cook up a pot of memories with one of these recipes.

## SOUPS

## Mom's Chicken Soup

*(the best cure for what ails you)*
*2 large chicken breasts,*
  *bone & skin on*
*Salt*
*Pepper*
*Olive oil*
*2 quarts chicken broth or stock*
*1 c. carrots, chopped into*
  *bite-size pieces*
*½ c. onion, chopped*
*1 c. celery, chopped into*
  *small pieces*
*2 c. egg noodles, wide*
*3 T. parsley flakes*

Wash chicken breasts, dry with paper towels, and rub with olive oil. Sprinkle salt & pepper on the chicken, place it on a cookie sheet and roast at 375 degrees for 40 minutes or until the chicken is cooked completely. Let the chicken cool, peel the skin off, and pull the chicken off the bone. Tear or cut the chicken into bite-size pieces.

In a large saucepan, heat the chicken broth and let it begin to simmer as you add the carrots, onions, celery, and noodles. Simmer for around 10 minutes, or until the noodles are cooked. Add the chicken and parsley. Continue to simmer for about 10 more minutes until the soup is completely heated.

## Simple Hamburger Vegetable Soup

1 lb. ground beef
½ c. onion, chopped
½ c. green pepper, chopped
4 c. beef broth
2 T. Worcestershire sauce
½ c. potato, diced
1 carrot, diced
1 c. whole kernel corn, frozen or
  canned (drained)
½ c. lima beans, frozen or canned
  (drained)
½ c. green beans, frozen or canned
  (drained)
1 - 14 ½ oz. can diced tomatoes
1 t. pepper
1 bay leaf

Brown ground beef, onion, and
pepper. Drain. Place in a large
saucepan or larger pot and add all
ingredients. Bring to just boiling;
reduce heat to medium and cover.
Simmer for 30 minutes, checking to
make sure all vegetables are tender.
Makes about 6 bowls of soup.
*Serve with salad or bread.*

*No salt was included because
the beef broth contains a good
bit of salt, unless you buy
low-sodium broth.*

## Chili

1 lb. ground beef
1 large onion, chopped
2 - 8 oz. cans crushed tomatoes
3 or 4 T. chili powder
  (depending on preference)
1 t. salt
1 t. sugar
2 - 8 oz. cans chili beans or
  red kidney beans

Brown ground beef and onion
together in a skillet. Meanwhile,
mix remaining ingredients in a large
pot. Drain meat and add to other
ingredients. Cover pot and simmer
chili for 30 minutes or up to
one hour.

Add more chili powder or hot
sauce if you desire a spicy chili.
*Serve in bowls with crackers, Fritos,
shredded cheese, chopped onions, or
the toppings of your choice.*

## White Chicken Chili

1 - 15 oz. can great northern beans
3 ¾ c. chicken stock
1 c. water
¾ c. onion, chopped
1 T. minced garlic
¼ t. salt
2 c. cooked, chopped chicken breast
1 - 4.5 oz. can green chilies
1 t. ground cumin
½ t. oregano

Place beans, chicken stock, water,
onion, garlic, and salt in a large
saucepan and bring to a boil. Cover
the pan, reduce the heat and simmer

for 45 minutes. Add the chicken, chilies, cumin, and oregano. Cover and simmer for 30 minutes. *Can top with sour cream, tortilla chips, and Monterey jack cheese, if desired.*

## Corn Chowder

*1 c. chopped onion*
*½ c. chopped celery*
*2 T. butter or margarine, melted*
*3 c. fresh or frozen corn, cut off cob*
*1 ½ c. potato, cut into small pieces*
*2 chicken flavored bouillon cubes*
*¼ t. pepper*
*¼ t. thyme*
*2 c. milk*
*1 c. half and half*

Cook onion and celery in butter in large saucepan until tender. Add corn and stir in the next 6 ingredients. Cover and simmer for about 15 minutes. Add the milk and half & half. Cook until the chowder is heated thoroughly, while continuing to stir.

## Broccoli-Cheese Soup

*1 - 10 oz. pkg. frozen broccoli, chopped*
*1 ½ c. milk*
*1 can cream of mushroom soup*
*2 T. butter*
*¼ t. pepper*
*1 c. shredded cheddar cheese*

Cook the frozen broccoli in a saucepan, following the package directions. Add the other ingredients and stir until combined. Simmer over medium-low heat until completely heated. Makes about 4 cups of soup.

## Beer Cheese Soup

*12 oz. light beer*
*6 slices bacon, cooked and crumbled*
*½ c. onion, chopped*
*½ c. celery, chopped finely*
*½ c. carrot, copped finely*
*¼ c. red sweet pepper, chopped finely*
*2 T. olive oil*
*1- 10 ½ oz. can chicken broth*
*¼ c. plain flour*
*1 c. half and half*
*3 c. med. cheddar cheese, shredded*

Open the beer and let it sit while you cut up all the vegetables. In a very large saucepan, sauté the onion, celery, carrot, and pepper in the olive oil until they are soft. Add the chicken broth and ½ of the beer to the vegetables. Using the last ½ of the beer, pour it into a mixing bowl and combine with flour, whisking it together until smooth. Slowly stir this into the broth mixture in the saucepan. Add the bacon, half & half, and cheese. Mix well by stirring, and heat until all the cheese is melted.

## Gina's Tortilla Soup

1 ½ t. olive oil

2 c. chopped onion

4 chicken breasts, cut into cubes
  before cooking

1 t. garlic, minced

½ t. cumin

2 T. lime juice (lemon will do,
  if lime isn't available)

1 t. chili powder

4 cans chicken broth

1 - 16 oz. jar Pace medium
  chunky salsa

2 c. frozen corn

Tortilla chips

Jack cheese

Sauté onion in olive oil until tender. Add chicken, and cook thoroughly in olive oil. Add garlic, cumin, lime juice, and chili powder just as chicken is cooked through. Add broth, salsa, and corn. *Serve over tortilla chips and garnish with Jack cheese.*

> *I live on good soup,*
>
> *not fine words.*
>
> **—MOLIERE**

## SERVE SIZZLIN' SANDWICHES.

Moms everywhere will tell you that, sometimes, simple is best. Two slices of bread and a piece of ham and cheese, and you're ready to go. On other days, though, the simple sandwich won't cut it. When you're craving a little more adventure between the slices, these recipes will come in handy. . .

### SANDWICHES

## Grilled Cheese

*(we'll start out simple)*

2 slices of bread, your favorite

1 slice of cheese, your favorite

Butter or margarine, softened

Spread butter on one side of each slice of bread. Place one slice, buttered-side down, into a warm skillet. Next add the cheese and top with the second slice of bread, buttered-side up. Turn sandwich until it is browned to your satisfaction. *Tastes even better with a bowl of soup! And eat those crusts— you're a grown-up now!*

## Reuben

*2 slices rye bread*
*1 slice Swiss cheese*
*¼ c. canned shredded*
    *sauerkraut, drained*
*3-4 slices corned beef*
*Thousand Island dressing*
*Butter*

Spread butter on one side of each slice of bread. Place the buttered-side down in a skillet over medium heat. Spread the Thousand Island dressing on one slice of bread. Place the Swiss cheese & corned beef on the other slice of bread. Using a fork, place enough sauerkraut to cover the bread over the dressing. Use a spatula to combine the sandwich. Continue heating & turning until both sides are grilled to suit you.

## Cuban Sandwich

*1 loaf Cuban bread*
*1 lb. smoked ham, thinly sliced*
*1 lb. roast pork, thinly sliced*
*½ lb. salami, thinly sliced (optional)*
*½ lb. Swiss cheese, thinly sliced*
*10-12 dill pickle slices,*
    *hamburger style*
*Lettuce*
*Sliced tomatoes*
*Mustard*

Cut Cuban bread into 4 pieces and then slice each piece lengthwise. Spread mustard on both sides of the bread. Layer ham, pork, and salami on one half of the sliced bread. Next, add Swiss cheese and pickles. Finally, add the lettuce and tomato slices and close the sandwich.

Warm the sandwiches in a skillet that has been sprayed with nonstick cooking spray. Just warm slightly on each side until the outside of the bread is toasty. (You can also warm the sandwiches on a grill with a lid). *For 1 sandwich, substitute the loaf of bread for a hoagie roll and buy smaller amounts of meats and cheese.*

## Club Sandwich

*3 slices of bread*
*2 slices of turkey*
*2 slices of ham*
*2 slices of roast beef*
*2 slice of cheese, your choice*
*2 slices of bacon*
*Mayonnaise*
*Lettuce*
*Tomato*

Toast the bread slices and spread the mayonnaise on each slice. Layer one half of each ingredient on one slice of bread. Top with a second slice of bread and continue layering with the remaining ingredients. Top with the final slice of bread.

**MOM-*sense*:** Cut the sandwich into triangles for easier eating.

## Pimento Cheese

1 - 8oz. pkg. extra sharp cheddar
cheese, shredded
1 - 8 oz. pkg. sharp cheddar cheese,
shredded
1 - 4 oz. jar pimentos, chopped
1/3 c. mayonnaise
Salt
Pepper

In a large bowl, mix the cheese with
the pimentos and then add the
mayonnaise. Salt and pepper to suit
your own taste. This can be stored
in the refrigerator in a covered
container for 1 week. *Serve on your
favorite bread as a sandwich, or
with crackers.*

## Delicious Burgers

*(When Jimmy Buffet sang, "I like
mine with lettuce and tomato,
Heinz 57 and French fried potatoes,
big kosher pickle and a cold draft
beer…" he had the right idea.)*

1 lb. ground chuck
   (use ground turkey if you prefer)
1 lb. ground sirloin
Salt
Pepper
Garlic powder
Worcestershire Sauce

Mix both meats well and pat into
burgers that are not too thick.
Sprinkle salt, pepper, and garlic
powder on both sides of burgers.
After seasoning, pour about 4 drops
of Worcestershire sauce on each
burger. Let patties sit and marinate
until ready to cook.

Grill, broil, or fry in a pan until
cooked to desired doneness. Serve
on a bun with lettuce, tomato,
cheese, pickles, mustard,
or mayonnaise.

## Sloppy Joes for Everyone

2 lb. ground beef or turkey
2 - 8 oz. cans tomato sauce
3/4 c. water
3 t. brown sugar
3 t. Worcestershire sauce
1/2 t. dry mustard
1 large onion, chopped finely
1/2 green pepper, chopped finely
Salt
Pepper

Brown meat and onion in a large
skillet and drain. Return meat to
skillet and add green pepper, tomato
sauce, and water. Stir well and add
brown sugar, Worcestershire sauce,
and dry mustard. Continue heating
over medium heat until mixture
thickens. Add salt and pepper to
taste. Serve on buns. *These may
remind you of summer camp. No
food fights, please!*

## SERVE DELICIOUS SIDES.

You have heard the expression "Behind every successful man, there's a good woman." Well, Moms know that behind every successful meat, there's a good side. Some of these sides are so good, they may steal the show from the main course!

## VEGETABLES & SIDE DISHES

## Mashed Potatoes

*2-3 pounds of red potatoes or*
  *Yukon gold potatoes*
*6-8 T. butter*
*½ c. milk*
*½ sour cream, if desired*
*Salt*
*Pepper*

Peel and large-chop or thickly slice potatoes. Cover with water and boil for 15-20 minutes, until tender. Just before you drain the cooked potatoes, heat the milk in a small pan over low heat or heat in the microwave for about 40 seconds. **(Do not boil the milk.)**

Place drained potatoes in a large mixing bowl and add the butter. Using an electric mixer, or a hand-held potato masher, begin mashing the potatoes. Slowly begin pouring the heated milk into the potatoes. (Be the judge of how much milk to add to the potatoes. Too much can result in runny mashed potatoes.) Add salt and pepper to taste.

## Green Beans

*(The Southern Way)*
*2-3 cans of green beans, drained*
  *or 5 c. of fresh green beans*
*1 onion, chopped*
*1 ½ c. chicken stock*
*Kosher salt*
*Pepper*

Place the green beans in a medium-large saucepan. Add onion and chicken stock. Sprinkle salt and pepper liberally on top. Cover and heat over medium heat for 1 hour. Remove lid and stir gently. Keep the lid off and continue heating about 15 more minutes if stock needs to reduce.

## Baked Beans

*2 - 15 oz. cans pork & beans, or*
*baked beans*
*1 medium onion, chopped*
*½ c. brown sugar*
*¼ c. ketchup*
*1 T. mustard*
*3 slices bacon*

In a large mixing bowl, mix all ingredients except bacon. Spray a 9 x 9 square baking dish with nonstick cooking spray, and add your bean mixture to the dish. Lay the bacon slices over the top of the beans. Bake at 350 degrees for 45 minutes.

**MOM-*sense*:** Add 1 chopped green pepper for even more flavor.

## Roasted Carrots

*8 carrots*
*1 ½ t. kosher salt*
*½ t. pepper*
*3 T. olive oil*

Peel carrots and slice them in half, diagonally. If they are especially thick, then slice them in half, lengthwise as well. (Just make sure that the sizes are similar so that they will cook evenly.) Place the carrots in a mixing bowl and add the other ingredients; toss until the carrots are well-coated.

Preheat the oven to 400 degrees. Place the carrots in one layer on a large baking sheet and roast them in the oven for about 20 minutes. They will be fabulous and are so easy!

**MOM-*sense*:** You can add some chopped fresh or dried parsley flakes, or dill to add flavor.

## Steamed Vegetables

*(the regular way)*
**Vegetables of your choice:**
*Green Beans, Yellow Squash, Zucchini Squash, Onion, Peppers, Asparagus, Broccoli, Carrots, and Cabbage are all good choices*
*1 T. butter*
*Salt*
*Pepper*

Vegetables should been washed and sliced into the desired size and shape you choose (strips, rounds,

etc.). Place the veggies in the top of a steamer basket. Sprinkle a little salt and pepper on top. You can also use other seasonings of your choice.

Fill the bottom pot with about 2 inches of water and bring to a simmer. *(Place lemon slices in the simmering water for extra flavor. You can try herbs, too.)*

When simmering, place the veggie basket on top, cover, and let the steam work its magic. Check for desired tenderness.

**MOM-*sense*:** Don't put too many vegetables in at one time. If they are too crowded, the cooking will not be even. Some will be mushy and some will still be raw.

## Steamed Vegetables

*(the super simple way)*
*Vegetables of your choice*
*1 T. butter*
*2 T. water*
*Salt*
*Pepper*

Wash vegetables and slice. Place into a shallow microwave-safe baking dish. Add water and butter. Sprinkle salt, pepper, and favorite seasonings on top. Cover with plastic wrap and microwave on HIGH 4-5 minutes. Stir and serve while hot.

## Easy Fried Rice

*3 c. rice, cooked and cold*
*2 T. olive oil*
*1 medium onion, chopped*
*1 - 16 oz. bag frozen vegetables*
*2 eggs, beaten*
*¼ – ½ c. soy sauce*
*Salt*
*Pepper*

In a large skillet, sauté the onion in olive oil until soft. Add the frozen vegetables and heat until they are somewhat thawed. Push to one side of the skillet and scramble the eggs on the other side. Stir the eggs and vegetables all together and sprinkle with salt and pepper. Add ¼ c. of soy sauce to the vegetables. Slowly spoon in the rice and mix entirely. Continue to cook until everything is steamy and hot. Add more soy sauce if you like. *Serve in bowls. (If you like meat in your rice, you can add cooked and chopped chicken, shrimp, pork, or beef.)*

## Homemade Macaroni & Cheese

*It takes a little longer than the boxed powder kind of mac & cheese, but it's worth it.*

*1- 8 oz. pkg. elbow macaroni*
*¼ c. butter*
*¼ c. plain flour*
*2 c. milk*
*1 t. salt*
*2 c. cheddar or American cheese, shredded*

Cook the macaroni according to the directions on the package. Drain and rinse well with hot water. Melt the butter in a large saucepan over low heat and add flour, whisking until it is smooth. Slowly add milk and cover over medium-low heat until thick and bubbling. Stir in the salt and cheese. Continue heating and stirring until the cheese melts. Mix the macaroni into the cheese sauce, and when well-blended, pour into a 9 x 9 square baking dish that has been sprayed with nonstick cooking spray. Sprinkle the shredded cheddar cheese over the top. Bake in a 350 degree oven for 30-40 minutes.

**MOM-*sense*:** I like to mix my cheeses for better flavor. Velveeta brand cheese is a good choice for the American cheese, because it melts so smoothly.

## MASTER MEMORY-MAKING MAIN DISHES.

Most all of us have a favorite meal. Whether yours is lasagna, chicken pot pie, or steak and potatoes, the memory of that meal is likely tied together with birthdays, grandparents, or special celebrations gone-by. We Moms find a particular delight in fixing that certain something that makes your heart smile. Here's hoping that you'll discover some new favorites (and memories) from these samplings . . .

## ENTREES & MAIN DISHES

### Aunt Peggy's Lasagna

*This lasagna recipe is fabulous and doesn't take a long time to prepare.*

½ pkg. lasagna noodles, 8 strips
2 T. olive oil
1 large onion, minced
1 t. minced garlic
2 lb. ground beef
2 ½ t. salt
½ t. rosemary
1 t. Italian seasoning
1 T. parsley
2 - 6 oz. cans tomato paste
1 ½ c. hot water
2 eggs, beaten
1 - 16 oz. cottage cheese or
   ricotta cheese
2 c. shredded mozzarella cheese
6 slices mozzarella cheese
Parmesan cheese

Heat oil in skillet and add onion and garlic. Cook until soft. Add beef and all dry seasonings. Cook meat until done and crumbly. Add tomato paste and hot water. Stir well, and simmer 15 minutes.

Cook noodles in large pot of salted water 10-12 minutes. Drain, and rinse well with cold water. Mix beaten eggs with cottage cheese.

To assemble in layers: Begin by putting a couple of spoonfuls of the meat sauce on the bottom of a 9 x 13 baking dish that has been sprayed with nonstick cooking spray. Then layer as follows: Noodles, cottage cheese mixture, sliced mozzarella cheese, meat sauce, and Parmesan cheese. Repeat again (except use shredded mozzarella cheese this time), ending with Parmesan cheese sprinkled generously all over the top.

Preheat oven to 350 degrees. Cover lasagna loosely with foil, and bake for 30 minutes. Uncover and bake 10 more minutes.

Let lasagna cool for about 10 minutes before serving. This will allow the lasagna to "set up," and it will be easier to cut and serve.

### Spaghetti

*(in 30 minutes or less)*
1 lb. ground beef or turkey
1 onion, chopped
2 t. minced garlic
Oregano
Italian seasoning
1 jar of spaghetti sauce or marinara
Pasta

Brown ground beef, garlic, and onion together. Drain well. Add to pot of waiting sauce. Sprinkle generously with oregano and Italian seasoning. Heat thoroughly over medium heat. Heat large pot of water that has been salted, and cook pasta while sauce is warming. *Serve over cooked pasta with salad and bread.*

## Quick and Simple Chicken Parmesan

*4-6 chicken cutlets*
*½ c. bread crumbs, Italian*
*½ c. grated Parmesan cheese*
*1 egg, beaten*
*2 T. olive oil*
*2-3 c. spaghetti sauce, your favorite*
*1 c. mozzarella cheese, shredded*

Mix the Italian breadcrumbs and Parmesan cheese in a bowl. Dip each piece of chicken into the beaten egg and then coat each side with the bread crumb/cheese mixture. Heat the olive oil in a large skillet over medium heat and place the chicken in the oil. Brown the chicken on each side. Pour the spaghetti sauce around the chicken and heat thoroughly. Sprinkle the mozzarella cheese on top of each piece of chicken. *Serve over hot pasta like spaghetti or angel hair with a green salad for a great meal.*

**MOM-*sense*:** If you can't find chicken cutlets in your grocery store, buy boneless, skinless chicken breasts and flatten them between 2 sheets of plastic wrap with your hand. If you use chicken breasts instead of cutlets, your cooking time will be a few minutes longer.

## Meatloaf

*2 lb. ground lean beef or turkey*
*2 slices bread, toasted crisp & cut or*
*   torn into small pieces*
*1 egg, beaten*
*¼ c. milk*
*1 onion, chopped*
*½ c. ketchup*
*Salt*
*Pepper*

Combine all ingredients well in a large mixing bowl. (You probably need to use your hands.) Form into a loaf and place in a 9 x 13 baking dish that has been sprayed with nonstick cooking spray. If you like, spread extra ketchup on top. Bake at 350 degrees for 45 minutes to 1 hour. Let cool for a few minutes before slicing. Serve with mashed potatoes and vegetables. *Leftover meatloaf slices make great sandwiches the next couple of days.*

**MOM-*sense*:** If your raw meatloaf mixture is dry, the finished product will be dry as well. Add a little more milk.

## Mom's Simple Pot Roast

1 beef chuck roast, approx. 4 lb.
Salt
Pepper
¼ c. plain flour
2 T. vegetable oil
2 large yellow onions, cut in half
8 peeled carrots or 3 c. baby carrots
4 c. small potatoes, cut in half

Preheat oven to 300 degrees.
Sprinkle salt and pepper over all of
roast. Put flour in a shallow dish or
bowl and dredge (coat) the roast in
the flour. Shake off the excess flour.

Heat the oil in a heavy, deep
casserole dish over medium-high
heat. Place the roast in and brown
it on all sides, about 3-4 minutes
per side. Remove the dish from the
heat; take the roast out and place it
on a plate. Put the onions, cut-side
down into the casserole dish. Now,
place the roast on top of the onions.
Cover the casserole dish with a lid or
aluminum foil and bake for 2 hours.

After 2 hours, add the carrots and
potatoes to the dish. Using a large
spoon, spread the juices over the
roast. Cover again and put it back
into the oven for 1-1 ½ hours, until
the meat is very tender. Carefully
remove the roast from the pan and
slice the beef with a serrated knife.
Serve with the potatoes and carrots.

## Pork Tenderloin

2 pork tenderloins, 1-1 ½ lb. each
1 c. soy sauce
1 c. sesame seeds
2 T. ground ginger
1 T. garlic powder
5 T. sugar
3 T. onion, chopped finely

Combine all the ingredients together,
except the pork, to make a marinade.
Place the pork into a container and
cover with marinade. Cover and
marinate 2-3 hours. Turn at least once.

Drain the marinade, but save it.
Bake the tenderloins in a shallow
baking dish that has been sprayed
with nonstick cooking spray for 1
hour at 375 degrees. Cool slightly
and slice into thin slices. Spoon the
reserved marinade over the pork
and serve.

## Roast Chicken

(Looks & sounds hard, but it's not!)
1 4-6 lb. chicken
1 lemon, cut in half
1 head of garlic, cut in half
1 onion, sliced into 4 thick slices
2 T. butter, softened
Salt
Pepper
*A bunch of fresh thyme inserted in
the cavity gives great flavor, but is
not necessary.

Begin by letting chicken sit on
counter for at least 30 minutes to

become room temperature. Rinse chicken inside and out under cold water. Pat the chicken dry with paper towels. Salt and pepper the chicken all over.

Stuff the lemon and garlic inside the chicken. Lay the 4 onion slices in two rows on the bottom of a roasting pan or a large baking dish. Place the chicken on top of the onions, breast side up. Rub the outside of the chicken with the softened butter. Sprinkle salt and pepper over the chicken again. Tie the legs of the chicken together with kitchen twine.

Preheat the oven to 425 degrees. Roast the chicken until the skin is golden brown and a meat thermometer reaches 165 degrees. Also, juices should run out clear if pierced with a fork.

Let the chicken sit for about 10-15 minutes before slicing. It is wonderful served with vegetables or sliced for sandwiches. *Roast chicken is perhaps the easiest and best-smelling food you will cook. Don't be surprised if it becomes a "new favorite."*

## Teriyaki Salmon

*2-4 salmon filets*
*Garlic salt*
*Brown sugar*
*Teriyaki sauce*

Place salmon filets into a glass-baking dish. Sprinkle with garlic salt. Cover with brown sugar and pour teriyaki sauce over all. Cover with plastic wrap and refrigerate for 2-3 hours. Spray grill with nonstick cooking spray. Place fish with skin side up on the grill. Cook 3-4 minutes, turn over and cook 3-4 more minutes. May need to cook longer if the filets are thick.

## Fried Chicken

*1 - 3-3½ lb. chicken, cut up*
*Salt*
*Pepper*
*2 c. plain flour*
*½ c. milk*
*2 eggs, beaten*
*Vegetable oil*

Wash chicken and dry with paper towels. Sprinkle salt and pepper all over each piece of chicken. Mix the eggs and milk together. Dip each piece of chicken into the milk/egg mixture. Have the flour in a gallon-size plastic zippered bag and put each piece of wet chicken in the bag and shake it until the chicken is coated in flour.

Place oil in large skillet until it is ½ full. Heat the oil over medium-high heat. Place no more than 4 pieces of chicken in the hot oil at one time. Cook the chicken until it is brown on all sides.

When chicken is done, place each piece on paper towels to drain.

MOM-*sense*: If you don't like all the chicken parts, don't buy a whole chicken. Buy only what you do like. Most grocery stores have chicken packaged by breasts, legs, thighs, and wings.

### Easiest & Most Delicious Baked Ham Ever

*Yes, you too can bake a ham with this simple recipe!*

1 - 3-3 ½ pound boneless,
  pre-cooked ham
1 c. Coca Cola, original
½ c. brown sugar

Heat your oven to 300 degrees. Use a 9 x 13 baking dish and completely cover the bottom with aluminum foil, using enough so you can cover the ham as well. Place the ham in the center of the pan. Rub the brown sugar over the ham and then pour the Coca-Cola over the brown sugar. Fold the aluminum foil together at the top of the ham and seal it all over.

Bake the ham 4 hours. Let it cool after removing it from the oven and before slicing it.

## DAZZLE WITH DESSERTS!

Whoever said, "Life's short. Eat dessert first" was on to something. Here are some treasures that come straight from Mom's sweet tooth. Enjoy!

### DESSERTS

### The Simplest Strawberry Shortcake

*2 pints of strawberries*
*Sugar*
*1 frozen rectangular pound cake,*
  *thawed*
*1 container whipped topping*

Wash and slice strawberries. Place strawberries in bowl and completely cover with sugar. Put strawberries in refrigerator for a couple of hours.

Slice pound cake into very thin slices. Place 2 or 3 slices of pound cake on a plate, spoon strawberries and juice over cake. Add a dollop of whipped topping. *Yum!*

### Chocolate-Dipped Strawberries

*2 pints fresh strawberries*
*1 - 6 oz. pkg. semi-sweet*
  *chocolate chips*
*1 T. shortening*

Rinse the strawberries and dry completely on paper towels. Set aside. (Make sure they are dry because the chocolate will not stick to wet strawberries.) Melt the chocolate and shortening in a microwave-safe bowl for 1 minute and stir. Continue heating in 30-second intervals until completely melted. Stir after each 30 seconds.

Hold strawberries by the stem and dip up to ½ of the berry into chocolate mixture. By dipping only half of the berry, the beautiful red will peek out above the yummy chocolate. Place the dipped strawberries on wax paper that has been placed on a cookie sheet. Chill until firm.

**MOM-*sense*:** Spray your bowl with nonstick cooking spray before melting chocolate. It will be easier to remove the chocolate and easier to clean!

## Apple Crisp
*(Friends will think you worked hard on this one.)*
*1 can apple pie filling*
*Brown sugar*
*Apple pie spice*
*Juice of 1 lemon*
*1 box white cake mix*
*1 stick butter, cut into pieces*

Pour apple pie filling into a glass pie plate. Top the pie filling with brown sugar and apple pie spice. Sprinkle lemon juice over all. Cover with ½ box of the cake mix. Place butter pieces all over the top. Bake at 350 degrees for 45 minutes. *Serve with a scoop of vanilla ice cream.*

## Fudge Pie
*(with no crust!)*
*1 stick margarine*
*1 square of unsweetened baking chocolate*
*2 eggs*
*½ c. plain flour*
*1 c. sugar*
*½ t. vanilla*
*½ c. chopped nuts, optional*

Melt the margarine and chocolate in a medium saucepan. Cool slightly. Add the other ingredients and stir well. Pour into a glass pie plate that has been sprayed with nonstick cooking spray. Bake at 325 degrees for 30 minutes. *Serve with a scoop of vanilla ice cream.*

## Super Delicious (and Easy) Hot Fudge Sauce
*1 stick margarine*
*1 c. sugar*
*¼ c. cocoa*
*¼ c. milk*

Melt ingredients in a small saucepan. Let boil for a little over one minute. *Serve over ice cream (with maybe a brownie) and enjoy!*

**MOM-*sense*:** If sauce is too thin, you didn't boil long enough. If it is too thick and chewy, you boiled too long. But once you find that magic minute, you'll never go back to Hershey's again.

## Simple Cherry or Apple Pie

*1 pkg. refrigerated pie crusts (2)*
*2 - 21 oz. cans cherry or apple*
*   pie filling*

Allow pie crusts to reach room temperature. Roll one piecrust onto a glass or metal pie plate. Add pie filling inside the crust. Unroll the second piecrust and lay it on top of the pie. Wrap the top piecrust edge around the bottom crust edge and seam together with your fingers. Pinch the edges together or mash with fork tines into the same shape around the entire pie. Cut 4 slits in the top piecrust to allow steam to escape. Cover the piecrust edges with aluminum foil and bake at 425 degrees for 40 minutes. Remove the foil after 30 minutes of baking time. Allow pie to cool at least 30 minutes before serving. *Serve with a scoop of vanilla ice cream.*

## No-Bake Chocolate Oatmeal Cookies

*1 stick butter*
*2 c. sugar*
*½ c. cocoa*
*½ c. milk*
*3 c. quick-cooking oats*
*½ c. peanut butter, creamy*
*1 t. vanilla*

In a large saucepan over medium heat, melt butter and stir in sugar and cocoa. Stir in milk and raise heat to bring mixture to a boil. Cook 1 minute, stirring constantly. Remove from heat and add oats, peanut butter, and vanilla. Mix very well and drop by spoonfuls onto wax paper. *Store in a covered container when cooled.*

## Miss Marie's Simple Peach Cobbler

*1 stick butter*
*1 c. sugar*
*1 c. self-rising flour*
*¾ c. milk*
*2 -15 oz. cans sliced peaches, heated*

Heat oven to 375 degrees. Place stick of butter into a 9-inch square baking dish and place in the oven until the butter melts. Put flour, sugar, and milk into a mixing bowl and beat with a mixer until well blended. NOW COMES THE TRICKY PART: DO NOT STIR FROM THIS POINT ON! Pour the flour, sugar, and milk mixture into the center of the melted butter. Next, gently pour the warm peaches into the center of everything. Bake for 30 minutes or until the pastry rises to the top and browns.

## Toll House Chocolate Chip Cookies

1 c. butter
¾ c. sugar
¾ c. dark brown sugar
2 eggs
2 ¼ c. plain flour
1 t. baking soda
½ t. salt
1 t. vanilla
2 ½ t. water
1 - 12 oz. pkg. semi-sweet
   chocolate chips

Cream the butter with both sugars and add the eggs until well beaten. Sift the flour, soda, and salt together. Add the dry ingredients to the sugar mixture. Add the vanilla and water and mix well. Add the chocolate chips and stir them into the mixture. Cover with plastic wrap and refrigerate for 30 minutes.

Heat the oven to 350 degrees. Place the cookie dough by spoonfuls onto a cookie sheet covered with parchment paper. Bake for about 10 minutes. Don't overbake or they will become too hard. Trust Mom, these are best if they are a little underbaked. *Enjoy with a glass of cold milk!*

## FIX SOMETHING FESTIVE!

*Rockin' around the Christmas tree is more fun while munching these treats!*

## A FEW HOLIDAY GOODIES

### Christmas Crunch

2 c. M & M plain candies
   (holiday colors)
2 c. Crispix cereal
2 c. Cheerios cereal
2 c. cocktail peanuts
2 c. pretzel sticks
1 ½ pkg. white chocolate baking squares (or almond bark), melted

Spray a very large mixing bowl with nonstick cooking spray and pour in first 5 ingredients. Pour melted chocolate over it and mix with a spatula or spoon that has been coated with nonstick cooking spray until everything is well coated. Pour mixture onto wax paper and spread into a thin layer. After candy hardens, break apart into small pieces and place in a zipper plastic bag or an airtight container.

**MOM-*sense*:** This is great to place in bags and give as gifts. People love it.

## Buckeyes

*(a tried and true*
*Christmas favorite)*
1 box confectioner's sugar, sifted
1 stick butter, melted
16 oz. peanut butter
4 T. milk
2 -12 oz. packages semi-sweet
   chocolate chips
3 T. shortening

Mix first 4 ingredients and roll into balls. Combine chocolate chips and shortening in a microwave-safe bowl and heat on medium power for 5 to 6 minutes. Stir to make sure chocolate is melted and not lumpy. Dip the balls into chocolate, leaving a bit of the peanut butter ball showing. Place onto wax paper for chocolate to harden. Store in airtight containers.

## Easy Boiled Custard

1 gal. milk
½ - ¾ c. sugar
2 lg. pkg. instant vanilla pudding
1 small pkg. instant vanilla pudding
1 t. vanilla
A pinch of salt

Mix all ingredients together with an electric mixer or a whisk until very smooth. Refrigerate until chilled.

   Serve with a dollop of whipped cream on top and a sprinkle of cinnamon.

## Peanut Butter & Chocolate Kisses Cookies

*These cute cookies are always a*
*favorite during the holidays.*

½ c. butter, room temperature
½ c. smooth peanut butter
¼ c. sugar
¾ c. brown sugar, firmly packed
1 egg
1 t. vanilla extract
¼ t. salt
1 ¾ c. plain flour
1 t. baking soda
3 T. sugar
48 Hershey Kisses, unwrapped

In a large bowl, beat the butter, peanut butter, sugar, brown sugar, egg, vanilla, and salt until fluffy and light. Add the flour & baking soda slowly until entire mixture is well blended. With your hands, shape the cookie dough into 48 round balls. Roll each one in the 3 T. of extra sugar. Place the balls 2 inches apart, on ungreased cookie sheets. Bake 8 to 10 minutes in a 375 degree oven that has been preheated. As soon as you remove the cookies from the oven, press a Hershey Kiss into the center of each cookie. Allow the cookies to cool.

**MOM-*sense*:** Unwrap the Hershey Kisses ahead of time, or while the first batch is in the oven. Otherwise, the baked cookies will harden while you're unwrapping.

# CHAPTER SEVEN

# Managing Your Money

*"Don't worry about not having a lot of money when you are starting out. You'll learn to be more creative."*

Money. What a very touchy, personal, and private subject. People are funny about their money. You'll be that way, too, one day. Might as well start today. After all, you will take care of and spend your money unlike anyone else. Your folks probably shared some tips with you about money matters, but you will chart your own course here. Everyone does.

Like I said before, money is personal. Because you are earning your own money now, you are probably thinking, "I can spend it any way I want." Well, of course you can, but taking a little advice in the area of personal finances is a wise thing to do.

## First things first: Budget, budget, budget!

All too often the word budget strikes fear in the hearts of people—in the same way words like *colonoscopy*, *taxes*, and *flossing* do. This is so unnecessary! Take it from Mom, just like vinegar, budgeting is our friend! In order for you to have any peace of mind about your finances, you really need to begin by keeping track of what money you have coming in and how much is going out through your spending. If you have no idea what either of these numbers are, you're going to be in big trouble sooner than you think. A budget can be the answer to your financial headaches. I know, planning a budget is a pain, and sticking to one is an even bigger pain. But as they say, no pain, no gain. And in the area of finances, the pain—and the gain—is worth it. Learning how to budget can save you some day.

Besides, creating a budget is really not as hard as you think. Since you are a young adult out in the world, you have not had time to accumulate a lot of debt and your budget listings should not be too difficult. This is a great time to start! Be sure to come up with a budget that makes sense for you and your money. Begin simply with a notebook and a pen. Draw a line down the center of a piece of paper. Label one side Income and the other side Expenses.

---

### SAMPLE BUDGET

**Income**
* Monthly salary
  (after taxes)

**Expenses**
* Rent
* Utilities
  electricity
  heat
  water
  phone
  Internet service
  cable
* Loans
* Credit card bills
* Car payments
* Insurance
* Groceries

Wow, it adds up pretty quick, doesn't it? Don't be overwhelmed. You may need to make different or less expensive choices, but you can handle this. Be realistic but honest with yourself, and eliminate expenses that you truly don't need to have. Making a budget and seeing where all your money goes is often a real eye-opener, but it can also be empowering when you realize that *you are in charge of your life and your own spending*. Self-control is always a good thing.

Another more up-to-date way to keep your budget is to use software programs. *Microsoft Money, Quicken,* or *Excel* are great tools to helping you keep your finances in check. They are not difficult and can make your record keeping paperless. Just don't forget to back them up.

# Don't spend more than you earn—or as Mom says: live within your means.

This is the part where the *common sense* is supposed to kick in: i.e., if you earn $100, you can't spend $200! Unfortunately, it is too common these days for people to spend more than they make (especially with credit cards and tempting "deals" like "no money down," or "no payments for twelve months!"). Not a good idea!

Don't start your independent life in debt. If you do, you will be digging out for longer than you think. Use the budget that you make and stick to it. You will have plenty of time later on to buy all those things you "need." There will always be things you want, but really don't need, so don't be influenced by pretty and shiny things. Learn to tell yourself no. Use your common sense and be smart enough to realize that you will be fine if you don't have the newest and best of everything.

**MOM'S RECOMMENDED READING FOR FINANCIAL KNOWLEDGE AND HELP**
+ *Financial Peace* by Dave Ramsey
+ *Pay It Down: From Debt to Wealth on $10 a Day* by Jean Chatzky
+ *The 9 Steps to Financial Freedom* by Suze Orman

**BE FRUGAL.**
Frugality may not be on your top-ten list of cool attributes, but remember it is severely underrated in our modern times. (Back in Ben Franklin's day, it was hip to be frugal!) It is quite all right to be a *tight wad* when you don't have a lot of money. In fact, it is more than all right. No one will ever fault you for watching your money—except maybe friends with higher incomes (or credit card bills) who want you to go out every night. If you don't have the funds for extras, be strong. To borrow a phrase from a former first lady, "Just Say No." If they are true friends, they will understand.

Being frugal is actually impressive. It simply means that you are smart, know what is important, and have the ability to delay gratification. It means you comprehend grown-up concepts like paying-the-bills-before-partying and making sure you have money saved up for emergencies instead of blowing every dime you have on a weekend trip or concert. In other words, it means you're *mature*. Be frugal and have a leg up on everyone else; you'll be the only one to know that you are saving by not spending more. Then you can laugh all the way to the bank.

> **MOM-*sense*:** Frugal doesn't equal boring; try to be creative when spending less. Sometimes a night in playing cards or watching a TV movie, or a day spent at the park is more fun than getting all dressed up to go out anyway!

### Tips for Being Frugal:
❖ Take a to-go cup of coffee from home instead of buying a $4 one at the corner shop.
❖ Pass on ordering expensive take-out and have a bowl of soup & a sandwich.
❖ Take leftovers to work for lunch a couple of days a week.
❖ Don't buy that new expensive suit in the window; look for comparable buys.
❖ Share and borrow books, movies, and music with friends when you can't afford new.

❖ Find a second-run movie theater and pay less to see that Hollywood blockbuster.
❖ Shop consignment stores; occasionally you'll find items with the tags still on.
❖ Turn off lights and appliances when you are not using them to lower your bills.
❖ Walk as many places as possible or carpool to save on gas.

## PAY WITH CASH.
My grandfather had a saying that went something like this, "If I don't have the cash, then I don't need to buy it." Now there's a statement seldom uttered today. In fact, buying and paying with cash is almost frowned upon if you judge by the credit card commercials on TV. News flash: cash is still the best way to go.

Paying with cash will assure you of never bouncing a check or having a hefty credit card bill. Paying with cash simply gives you peace of mind. If you pay with cash, you have the confidence of knowing that the item you purchased is actually yours at the time you got it. Trust Mom, you will be much happier and sleep better at night knowing that the things you have are paid for.

## BE VERY CAREFUL WITH CREDIT CARDS.
Boy oh boy, are those little pieces of plastic tricky. On one hand, credit cards can be wonderful tools to have

## MIND YOUR CREDIT CARDS

**What a credit card is for:**

✓ Emergencies like flat tires, illness, or lost bags on an airplane

✓ Ordering from a catalog or online

✓ To establish a good credit rating, i.e., by paying the balance in full and on time

✓ To pay for business expenses and then be reimbursed

**What a credit card is NOT for:**

✗ To pay your bills because money is a little tight this month

✗ To fill your closet with a new wardrobe because "you have nothing to wear"

✗ To buy gifts for other people (your friends don't want you to go in debt for them)

✗ To "show off" by buying dinner or drinks for a group of people

---

if you really need them, and on the other hand, they can be the absolute worst things to ever happen to you. In some ways, owning a credit card is like owning a boa constrictor; it is okay as long as you set proper boundaries. (Let it run free, though, and it might squeeze you to death!) Of course, Mom knows that you need a credit card. Mom also knows that you need to be very careful when you get one.

You will probably receive an offer for a credit card in the mail weekly, if not daily. Shred them immediately, especially those proclaiming, "FREE" all over them. Honey, nothing in this world is free! You will also be bombarded with this offer, "Sign up for a credit card with us today and get 10% off your purchase," in just about every store you shop. Well, what they don't tell you is, if you

don't pay that balance in full when the bill comes, you will be charged 20% (or more) of your balance each month until you pay it off.

On the subject of store credit cards, you need to know that these can cause serious financial problems down the road. Just say *no* and get in the habit of saying *no* to the sales clerks who offer those perks to you. Those credit cards sound like a good idea at the time, but they will pile up and you'll find yourself barely paying the minimum balance because you have so many. You don't need that Old Navy jacket for five-dollars-less-with-a-new-credit-card; wait until you can afford it, and pay cash.

If you do have a credit card you are having trouble paying off and are often just paying that minimum balance, beware of the finance charges. You can pay the minimum and still have next month's statement be more than last month's if the service charge is extremely high. Just beware!

**MOM-*sense*:** Don't ever think of skipping a payment just because the minimum payment says $0 due. You will pay more in the long run.

## BALANCE YOUR CHECKBOOK.

Balancing your checkbook—is it really that important? You bet it is. If this is a task that you have not yet mastered, now is the time for a simple, crash course in checkbook balancing. It isn't rocket science, just discipline: the key to keeping your checkbook balanced is to *write down every single transaction you have.* This includes ATM withdrawals, deposits, and checks that you write.

Don't ever forget to jot down the amount of a check you write, cash you withdraw, or deposit that you make. And, for heaven's sake, keep your balance current. Do it as you write down the transaction. Get yourself a pencil and keep your running balance written in pencil, because just as sure as it will rain one day, you will make a mistake. If you have written your balance in pencil, it is easily corrected. I realize that using a pencil in this day and age may sound primitive, but trust Mom, it still works.

## Glossary of Checkbook Terms:
**Number** – The number that is at the top right-hand side of your check
**Date** – The date your transaction occurred
**Transaction Description** – Either the company or person to whom your check was written; a withdrawal at an ATM machine or bank, or a deposit
**Payment** – The amount of the check you wrote, or a withdrawal
**"X" Column** – Place to mark when a transaction has cleared your account
**Fee** – Any fee your bank charges you, i.e., NSF fees, service charges, or penalties
**Deposit** – The amount of money you deposit into your account
**Balance** – The exact amount of money you have in your account at any given time

## UTILIZE ONLINE AND FEE-FREE BANKING.

Most banks and financial institutions are now technology-friendly and have online banking available for their customers. Online banking is fairly easy to use and basically instantaneous when it comes to having your transactions posted. For instance, if you use a checking account debit card at a grocery store, it will more than likely be posted to your account before you arrive home and begin putting the food away.

## SAMPLE CHECK REGISTER

| No. | Date | Transaction Description | Payment | Fee | Deposit | BALANCE |
|-----|------|------------------------|---------|-----|---------|---------|
|     |      |                        |         |     |         | 764.84  |
| 425 | 7/11 | Whole Foods            | 39.52   |     |         | -39.52  |
|     |      |                        |         |     |         | 725.32  |
| ATM | 7/11 | Cash Withdrawal        | 40.00   |     |         | - 40.00 |
|     |      |                        |         |     |         | 685.32  |
| Dep. | 7/13 | Deposit (payroll)     | 689.93  |     | +689.93 |         |
|     |      |                        |         |     |         | 1375.25 |
| 426 | 7/14 | City Water Dept        | 27.51   |     |         | -27.51  |
|     |      |                        |         |     |         | 1347.74 |
| 427 | 7/14 | Silver Lake Apt (rent) | 675.00  |     |         | -675.00 |
|     |      |                        |         |     |         | 672.74  |
| SC  | 7/15 | Bank Service Charge    |         | 12.00 |       | -12.00  |
|     |      |                        |         |     |         | 660.74  |

Online banking is a terrific way to stay abreast of everything going on in your accounts. You can log on at any time and see exactly where your account stands. You can also look for a check that you have been waiting to see clear and know if you are in trouble because you forgot to post some transactions. You should even have the ability to transfer money between accounts and pay your bills. Give it a try!

One other handy bit of information about banking is to find a bank that charges the least possible amount of fees. I know it seems crazy for a bank to charge you to keep your money, but they do. You can "bank shop" for the best deals just like you do for everything else. Don't settle on the biggest or best-known bank; look around and compare. They do need your business. Also, ask about minimum balances in accounts that you have. There are different rules for those as well.

**MOM-*sense*:** It is a good thing to be private when dealing with money matters. Don't ever leave your bank records lying around for anyone else's eyes to see. Be careful when making financial transactions at an ATM, a grocery store, or the mall. Be discreet, and always, always save all your receipts!

## GO AHEAD AND BUY THE INSURANCE.

Something that you need to look into now is insurance. Some of you may be lucky and blessed enough to have had parents who took care of insurance for you. Others may have already been at least paying for auto insurance. Well, guess what? Now, it is your turn to pay for your own insurance.

If you drive your own vehicle, you will need auto insurance. In fact, many states don't allow you to have a driver's license without it. Mom says definitely get yourself some auto insurance. Auto insurance is so necessary. If you have an accident, you'll be glad you have insurance. Shop around when buying insurance because some companies are definitely less expensive than others. Also, buy from a reputable company.

Mom also recommends that you have health insurance. It can be a little costly, but if you are sick, you'll be glad you have it. Healthcare is extremely expensive, as are medications. Health insurance will offset those costs and be a blessing to have. So, buy the insurance.

### SAVE FOR A RAINY DAY.

Mom agrees with Old Ben; you never know when an emergency will pop up, so you need to be prepared. Emergencies never seem to let us know when they are coming, and they often show up at the most inconvenient times. If you do nothing else responsible with your money, at least have an emergency account ready and waiting. Hopefully you will never need it, but you never know . . .

*"A penny saved is a penny earned."*
**—BENJAMIN FRANKLIN**

Experts say that an emergency account should have at least three months of your salary in it. Just in case your emergency is a health-related situation and you can't work, you would be able to live for a while. Keep your emergency account on your priority list and add to it often. Also, don't touch it just because you haven't had an emergency in a while—and a cruise to Jamaica is not an emergency! Remember the Boy Scout motto (even if you aren't one): "Always Be Prepared."

### PAY YOUR BILLS ON TIME AND ESTABLISH A GOOD CREDIT RATING.

Make a habit of paying your bills on time. Hey, even pay them a little early if you can. Sit down when those bills come in, look at your bank balance, check your budget for the month, and determine if you can pay it early. Do not make a habit of seeing how much you can spend before your bills are paid. You will regret it, and your credit rating will suffer.

Your credit rating is the one single thing in this world that can make or break you if you become a procrastinator in the bill-paying department. Trust Mom, if you pay your bills late, the company will report you to the Credit Bureau. Once you have a bad credit rating, it is there for all businesses to see, and it is hard to clean it up . . . think of it as a grown-up report card.

Your credit "report card" will be checked when you apply for a job, an apartment, or a loan for that first house or dream car. Your credit scores and your credit history will be accessed by financial institutions to determine how much risk you may be. If you have low credit scores and bad credit history, you will most likely pay higher interest rates than normal, or you could be turned down completely. How devastating would that be?

Check your credit report before you apply for any jobs, loans, or any type of housing. Mommy and Daddy can't always be your back-up; you will need to rely on your own reputation. Credit reports can have mistakes on them, so look carefully. Most states have credit bureaus that you can check, or you can look online for other choices.

Another helpful strategy for paying bills is to use an automatic bill pay option through your bank or financial institution. This handy method makes sure that your bills are paid on time and doesn't require much effort from you. (Except for that very important fact of depositing your paycheck into your account.) If you like to be very organized, you will love this way of paying your bills.

## KNOW THE DIFFERENCE BETWEEN A "NEED" AND A "WANT"—AND DON'T WANT EVERYTHING YOU SEE!

Only shop when you truly need something. In case you're not sure what exactly a "need" is, let Mom remind you:

*Deodorant = Need*
*Latest NFL computer game = Want*
*Electricity (unless you're Daniel Boone) = Need*
*Electric Guitar = Want*
*Haircut = Need*
*Glitzy New Hair Accessory = Want*

Got that straight? Good. (If you're still confused, just know that 97 percent of the things we see on TV commercials and in magazine ads are Wants; and everything that the people *don't* have in the third-world countries featured on *National Geographic* are Needs.)

When you are shopping and you find something you want to buy, take a Moment to think about how long you had to work to cover the price of it. If you look at it that way, it often doesn't seem worth it. (Is that new pair of boots really worth three days' work?) Don't make a habit of window-shopping and mall browsing just to kill time. Often when you do this, you wind up carrying out bags of things you may not really need.

Trust Mom, limit your "browsing time," or you will be sitting at home with shopping bags full of things that you don't really need after blowing your bank balance. If you are feeling buyer's remorse, go ahead and return those items and save your sanity. Just because things look good in a window or on a mannequin doesn't necessarily mean they need to be hanging in your closet or sitting in your kitchen. Use your common sense here!

## SEVEN QUESTIONS TO ASK YOURSELF BEFORE BUYING ANYTHING

(taken from one of Mary Hunt's "Debt-Proof Living" newsletters off www.cheapskatemonthly.com)

*In the heat of a shopping experience, Mary says to remove yourself from the store (or the computer if you're shopping online) for a Moment to ask yourself these questions:*

**1.** Do I need it, really?

**2.** Could this be considered by any reasonable person to be a planned purchase?

**3.** Will this make my life better, or add to the chaos or clutter?

**4.** Don't I already have something that will do just as well?

**5.** Do I have the cash to pay for it right now?

**6.** If I walk away from this purchase, how will I feel a month from now?

**7.** Am I willing to sleep on my decision for 48 hours?

## SEARCH FOR GOOD VALUES AND FIND DEALS.

When you do shop, shop for quality, not price. Buy the best that you possibly can. Moms will tell you buying quality simply means that you understand that well-made things are going to last longer. They don't break as easily, because they are usually stronger. Buying items of better quality may save you money in the long run because you won't need to replace them as you would a cheaper, less well-made item.

**MOM-*sense*:** Buy in bulk! Stock up on items that you use a lot by buying in bulk when you are shopping. Paper towels, light bulbs, toilet paper, and anything else you go through quickly are all cheaper to buy in larger quantities.

To find the best deals, read newspapers and advertisements. Often you will find what you are looking for with a little research. Compare prices between stores on items that you need to buy. Some stores will match a lower price from another store. It does pay to look around and not buy at the first place you look. You can save yourself some money and be proud of your detective skills at the same time.

**MOM-*sense*:** Remember, even if something is heavily discounted, it is not a "deal" if you don't have the money to pay for it! (You can still ring up debt buying clothes at 50 percent off!)

### CUT BACK AT HOME AND SAVE SOME CASH.

Clearance aisles and consignment shops aren't the only way to save money. You can also save money by saving energy. Utility bills are a fact of life, and they can fluctuate (and even skyrocket) depending on your habits.

**Ways to Earn Extra Money**

Sometimes, you must be willing not only to sacrifice, but also to work harder. When cutting your spending isn't enough and you need to have some more money coming in, here are some ideas:

✳Get a second (or first) job—babysit, tend bar, wait tables, deliver food, tutor, work in retail on weekends.

✳Get a roommate and cut down on expenses.

✳Find a cheaper place to live, and move.

✳Look for a higher paying job.

### TIPS TO CUT DOWN ON HIGH UTILITY BILLS

**Refrigerator:** Don't leave that door open while you are making a sandwich.

**Hot water:** Everyone likes a hot shower or bath, just don't overdo it. Shorten your time in the tub or under the stream and lower the bill.

**Fireplace:** Close the damper if you aren't using it.

**Leaky faucets:** Have them repaired immediately, or do it yourself with a few tips from your local hardware or home improvement store.

### In the Wintertime:

**Heat:** Lower the thermostat when you leave for work. So it might be a little cooler when you get home; you'll survive.

**Curtains, shades, or blinds:** Keep them open, so that while the sun is out, it will warm your home. Close at night to keep the warmth in.

### In the Summertime:

**Air Conditioning:** Raise the thermostat temperature as much as you can tolerate. If you keep it below 70 degrees all the time, you'll be "cool as a cucumber," but you will soon receive a hefty bill in the mail. Especially take it up a couple of degrees when you leave for the day.

**Curtains, shades, or blinds:** Keep them closed when it is hot outside. It will keep the inside cooler.

> *"The holy passion of Friendship is oh so sweet and steady and loyal and enduring a nature that it will last through a whole lifetime, if not asked to lend money."*
> — **MARK TWAIN**

## REALITY CHECK:
# Don't borrow from your family & friends, and don't loan money to family & friends.

It's sad, but true: one of the hardest lessons that you will ever learn involves money and family or friends. It may not seem that way now, but money owed to people we love is a very sticky subject. Don't ever borrow money that you do not intend to pay back on a timely basis (even from your Mom!). On the chance that you do borrow, be prepared for problems if you don't pay it back soon. If a relative or friend has the unenviable chore of reminding you of what you owe, you will begin to avoid that person, you'll both feel awkward, and worst of all, you will lose their trust. If you can't pay on the schedule that was intended, let that person know immediately.

If you feel compelled to make a loan to a friend or family member, make sure you are clear whether it is a loan or a gift. Keep communication lines open between you and the borrower. Typically, you will write a check for a loan, so be sure to jot "LOAN" on the memo line. Then, you will have documentation of the transaction. Above all, don't expect too much, and you won't be disappointed. Hard times come, and chances are, if someone has borrowed money from you, they probably weren't in the best financial shape to begin with. (For large amounts, suggest a bank or lending institution.)

To summarize this delicate topic, no one ever wants to be taken advantage of, and you shouldn't take advantage of others, either. Just remember this when dealing with money matters and family or friends. Always be gracious and remember that even though money isn't worth losing relationships over, it happens.

## BE LIKE THE MAGI: GIVE GIFTS WISELY.

You don't need to spend a small fortune on the gifts that you buy. You are at the beginning of your life, not the end, and you have lots of people in your life, all with birthdays, plus a zillion other special occasions. So be thoughtful, not crazy. Gift-giving represents a feeling toward another person more than anything else, and it should be considered as such. Moms know better than anyone that homemade and heartfelt gifts are always the best. A gift doesn't have to be expensive to be "just right."

When giving gifts, put a good deal of thought into it. Consider the recipient and what is important to them. No one that is special to you would ever want you to spend too much money on a gift that would break your bank. Be creative and clever when giving gifts to people close to you. They will appreciate your thoughtfulness and treasure your generosity.

## MAKE IT A PRIORITY TO DONATE AND TO TITHE TO YOUR CHURCH.

Donations are probably not heavy on your mind since you are just getting started in your independent life. Even though you may not be bringing home a huge salary just yet, you can still donate on a small scale. Donating to the charity of your choice has benefits. Not only do you bless someone else and receive the blessing of giving, you can also deduct your donation from your taxes when you file your income tax.

If you are a regular attendee of a church or religious institution (and Mom hopes you are), you are well acquainted with tithing. Tithing is typically known as giving 10 percent of what you earn to your church. Many people follow this practice and are faithful givers. However, it can be difficult when you are a newly independent person. Give what you can and don't feel pressured, especially when you are having trouble making ends meet. Someday you will be able to give more.

### Gifts that Give without Breaking the Bank:

* Photos in inexpensive, but unique frames
* A home-cooked meal, presented creatively
* A fun magazine or inexpensive subscription
* Personalized stationery or monogrammed items
* Making a creative card that tells the person what you like about them
* Combining resources with another person/persons to buy a gift
* Making a CD mix of honoree's favorite songs
* Doing your loved one's least favorite (and most avoided) chore

# Know how to tip.

We all love good service when we go out, and want to be treated well. The way you show appreciation for good service is to tip the server. Years ago, tipping was done in only a few places, but it seems like these days, everyone has their hand (or their tip jar) out.

The first profession that comes to mind when you talk about tipping is restaurant servers. Waiters and waitresses don't make the minimum pay wage and rely on tips to make up the difference in pay. Tipping is a personal choice. Just remember to be fair.

## STANDARD TIP AMOUNTS

**Restaurant server** – 15-20% for good service, 10% for bad service & speak to manager

**Bartender** – $1 per drink or 15% of bar bill

**Washroom attendant** – $1 for towels, gum, lint brush

**Coat check** – $1 per coat

**Doorman** – $1 for hailing a cab or helping with bags

**Valet (car)** – $2 for getting your car

**Parking garage** – $2 for getting your car

**Taxi driver** – 15% of fare or more if he helps with luggage

**Airport skycap** – $1-$2 per bag, $3 if it is extremely heavy

**Deliveries** – Food deliveries $2-$4. Also tip for grocery & dry cleaning deliveries

**Hairdresser** – 15-20% for haircuts. For extras like perms & color, that can be very expensive, so use your own judgment.

**Shampoo person** – $2

**Spa services** – 15% for manicures, pedicures, massages, wax, & facials

**Room service** – 15%

**Bellhops** – $1-$2 per bag they carry

**Hotel maids** – $2-$3 per day in a nice hotel

**Concierge** – $5-$10 for the services he/she performs

**Building staff** – Holidays – Superintendent $30-$50

**Doorman** – $25-$40

**Elevator operator** – $20-$30

**NO TIP** – Places that say "no tips"; bartenders or servers at private parties; professionals like accountants, doctors, and lawyers; flight attendants; ushers in a theater; service professionals like plumbers and electricians

*One more thought about tips:* Use your own judgment in places where a *tip jar* is sitting on a counter. I am not often inclined to give someone a tip that poured me a cup of coffee or handed me a sandwich through a drive-through window. It's your money, and you can choose how you spend it and give it.

## LAST BUT NOT LEAST: FILE YOUR TAX RETURNS ON TIME!

Never forget this date for as long as you live: **APRIL 15**. It's my Aunt Ruth's birthday. No, just kidding: it is the day that your Federal Income Tax Return is due. You can take comfort in the fact that it will always be the day that your Federal Income Tax Return is due. You know the old line about death and taxes? Well, taxes are not going away, so get used to them. You may not need a Certified Public Accountant to help you file your return, but make sure you understand everything before you sign your name on the line and put it in the mail. And if it's just too complicated for you to understand, call Mom—I'll hand the phone to Dad for you.

## KEEP THESE FOR EASIER TAX RETURN FILING:

* ✳ W-2 form and any 1099 forms
* ✳ Bank statements
* ✳ Investment statements
* ✳ Medical records and receipts
* ✳ Receipts for large purchases
* ✳ Credit card statements
* ✳ Receipts for any deductions, including donations, etc.
* ✳ Records for home ownership and any improvements

**I am what you call an "impulse buyer." What can I do to reign in my spending?**

Well, first write down a copy of those seven questions to ask before buying anything, and keep it in your purse or car. And second, LEAVE THE CREDIT CARDS AT HOME! You'll bring home fewer shopping bags if you pay with cash.

**How do I avoid identity theft?**

Shred, shred, shred! Don't be the target of identity theft. Shred all of your financial documents when you no longer need them. Also, it is a good idea to shred any papers that have your name and address on them.

**Is it all right to use other banks' ATM machines?**

Sure it is—if you don't mind paying an extra fee! Make sure you know what the fee is for using an ATM machine that belongs to a bank other than yours. *There will be a fee!* Sometimes, though, when you're in a bind, that $2.50 charge is worth it.

## Just one more thing . . .

★**Beware of "sales."** Never buy anything simply because it is on sale. As my dad used to say, "It's not how much you've saved that worries me." You'll soon learn that stores have their "best sale ever" every other week. Only buy if you really need it.

★**Beware of "picking up the tab."** Don't offer to pay the tab for the group on your credit card and have them hand you cash, especially if you're broke. The bill will still come, and chances are the cash will be gone by then!

★**Hang on to those receipts.** Always keep your credit card receipts for purchases until the bill comes. Compare the two and make sure you are only being charged for what you bought. Also, be sure to ask for a gift receipt if you are buying a gift. Some stores have pretty strict return policies!

★**Keep your money matters to yourself.** Once you are out of college and no longer a student, you are considered an adult, and it is tacky to talk about how broke you are.

# CHAPTER EIGHT

# Personal Appearance, Clothes, and All That Jazz

*"You never get a second chance to make a first impression."*

We live in a culture that puts a premium on appearance. Good looks and fashion know-how open doors, influence people, and advance careers faster than you can say Paris Hilton. Well, Mom's here to tell you that, no matter what Hollywood or *Vogue* magazine says, the long-worn phrases "it's what's inside that counts," "pretty is as pretty does," and "don't judge a book by its cover" are still as true as ever! Today's hot babe is tomorrow's wrinkled old woman, so concentrate on what lasts!

Having said that, there's nothing admirable in being a slob. And the old expression "you never get a first chance to make a first impression" is also true as ever. God created you special, Mom molded and polished you, so go ahead and be the best you that you can be!

## First things first: By all means, groom yourself.

Every single day, without fail, you should practice good hygiene. Shower or bathe, brush your pearly whites, scrub your face clean, use deodorant, and go about your day smelling and looking good. Whether you are male or female, if you're "looking for love" or too busy to bother, take good care of yourself. The old adage is true that you feel better when you've made an effort to look better. I'm not talking get-up-at-5-to-put-your-fake-eyelashes-on-and-drink-your-green-tea-and-file-your-toenails better; I just mean be neat and clean and look your best.

Good basic hygiene doesn't have to be costly. Plain, old-fashioned soap and water does wonders for sweat and dirt. If you already have a "cleansing regimen," feel free to skip the following list, but for those who want a "refresher" course (pun intended), read on:

**Skin** – Wash daily and moisturize. Use a milder soap or cleanser for your face. Wear sunscreen and take especially good care of your face. It's the only one you've got, and your Mom loves it. Also, don't forget a good deodorant. You don't ever want to be "that guy (or girl) with B.O."

**Shaving** – *Guys:* Shave daily or go for that stubble look. If you keep a beard, goatee, or mustache, keep it trimmed neatly.

*Girls:* Shave your legs and armpits often, even more often in the summer. For unwanted hair on the face or other places, try waxing at a local beauty spa. It is not very expensive and lasts a good while.

**Teeth** – Brush at least three times a day. Don't forget to use dental floss. If you want whiter teeth, try some of the teeth whitening strips for sale in grocery or discount stores. They are much improved, work fairly well, and are much cheaper than whitening in a dental office.

**Hair** – Keep your hair washed and clean on a daily basis. It is a great idea to keep a haircut that you can manage and style without too much trouble. Make sure the cut is flattering for you. And be wary of you or a friend spontaneously deciding to cut your own hair. You may be better off paying someone who was trained. If by chance you should happen to get a bad haircut (it happens to the best of us), move on after a brief "mourning" period: It will grow back.

**MOM-*sense*:** Have an "emergency accessory" (scarf, ballcap, or clip) available for those bad-hair days that are bound to come now and then.

**Makeup** – Don't ever wear too much. You don't want to be accused of looking like a clown—or something worse. Tasteful, well-applied, minimal makeup is the way to go. If you are unsure about how to apply makeup properly, make an appointment at a cosmetic counter in a department store. Often they will do a makeover for free and teach you how to apply items. Of course, they will count on you to purchase some of their products afterward; just check the prices first, and buy that twelve-dollar tube of lipstick if that's all you can afford.

**Perfume/Cologne/Aftershave** – Mom has one failsafe piece of advice relating to this subject: *Easy does it!* You've probably been around people who went a little overboard with the smelly stuff, so you know what I mean. Don't be a walking Estee Lauder counter. A good rule of thumb to remember is this: "One spray goes a long way." If your smell precedes and follows you and nauseates those you meet, you will offend people. And keep in mind that more people today have allergies and react by sneezing and sniffing. Ask your friend or roommate to judge whether you're coming on too strong. You could ruin a good relationship with too many drops of perfume, cologne, or aftershave.

**Nails** – Keep your fingernails clean and trimmed neatly. If you are a biter, bless your soul. Try to stop if you can. For those unsightly toenails, keep them clean too, and trim them every couple of weeks or so.

## SPLURGES WHEN YOU HAVE SOME EXTRA CASH . . .

**Manicures and pedicures** – Nothing feels better than a manicure and pedicure. If you can only do one, go for the pedicure and clean your own nails.

**Facials** – A facial is heavenly and makes your skin glow.

**Massage** – Heaven on earth. Go for the Swedish and enjoy. You might just fall asleep.

## EMBRACE YOUR OWN STYLE.

No doubt you've seen the latest looks in fashion magazines and on television shows. So you probably have some idea of what is *in style* at the Moment. The only problem with what is *in style* (besides the fact that it may be outlandishly expensive and only look right on size 0 supermodels) is that *your style* may not match it. Never fear, because the majority of the world is in the same boat with you, and guess what? It's okay.

*Your style* is really the only thing that is important when it comes to how you dress and what you choose to buy. As I mentioned, more than likely the *in style* items either don't fit your body type or are way too expensive for your budget. Having your own style says a lot about you. It shows that you have confidence in your choices and that you are your own person.

Dress as if today is important. We've all been told by our Moms to make sure we have on clean underwear. As a kid, I always was afraid that meant that someone was going to check my underwear and that I would be forbidden to do something because my underwear wasn't up to par! Now I know it simply means to always be dressed properly and in clean clothes in case something were to happen—good or bad. Be prepared.

Dressing is a choice, a conscious choice that we all make. Mom knows that people who dress as if today is an important day are actually treated better and generally looked at differently. You know the people I'm talking about. They look "put together," like they can handle anything. Be aware that with a little extra time and effort, you could be one of these people.

Fair or not, other people are going to judge you by what you wear. Having said that, I don't want you to go around comparing yourself or worrying about what others think about how you're dressed. Just don't make a habit of wearing your old worn-out high school track team

## Must-Have-in-Closet Checklist

**FOR GUYS:**

Sport Coat

Dark Suit

Dress Pants

Casual Pants like Khakis

Dress Shirts

Button-Down Shirts

Collared Cotton/Knit Shirts

3 or 4 great Ties (at least 1 conservative)

Jeans

Rain Jacket

Heavy Winter Coat

Lightweight Jacket

Nice Dress Shoes

Casual Loafers

Boots

Tennis Shoes/Athletic Shoes

Flip Flops or Slip-on Casual Shoes

**FOR GIRLS:**

Great Black Dress

Good Fitting Jeans

Black Pants

Good Skirt in black and khaki

Blouses or Shirts/dressy and casual

Casual collared cotton/knit Shirts

Cardigan Sweater in solid color

Sweaters for cold and warm weather

Rain Jacket

Heavy Winter Coat

Lightweight Jacket

Good Black Pumps

Sandals

Cute Flats

Tennis Shoes/Athletic Shoes

Boots

Flip-Flops

Slip-on Casual Shoes

Good Black Purse

sweat pants everywhere you go. Wear them to sleep in, or on a lazy weekend day at home.

Buy clothing that fits you and that you can afford. Rather than follow every new fad, it's smart to buy some good quality basic pieces of clothing that you can mix and match and wear often. Make the best choices for your body type and for your station in life. If you are still in school, your choices will probably be more casual. If you are working, you may lean toward more professional attire.

> **MOM-*sense*:** No matter what you're wearing, you always look better with a smile.

## DRESS APPROPRIATELY FOR APPOINTMENTS AND EVENTS.

Mom remembers the days when riding an airplane was an occasion to get dressed up, and when the doctor who saw you in the waiting room wore a suit and tie instead of scrubs. Alas, those well-dressed days are over, but that doesn't mean you can look like a slob wherever you go. Here's hoping the following chart helps you know *what* to wear *when*.

## Job Interviews

**FOR GUYS:**
Sport coat, button-down shirt, tie, dark or khaki pants, clean shoes

**FOR GIRLS:**
Jacket or conservative blouse or sweater, skirt or nice pants, nice shoes, minimal jewelry

## Weddings

**FOR GUYS:**
*Day wedding* – Sport coat and nice pants, shirt, and tie
*Night wedding* – Dark suit, shirt, and tie
*Black Tie/Formal* – Rent a tux, boys, and enjoy it
*Black Tie Optional* – Suit or tux

**FOR GIRLS:**
*Day wedding* – Dress, skirt, or nice pants and top
*Night wedding* – Cocktail dress
*Black Tie/Formal* – Cocktail dress either short or long; very dressy pants and top

## Funerals

**FOR GUYS:**
Dark suit, always. If you don't have one, a dark sport coat will do with a shirt and tie.

**FOR GIRLS:**
Dark dress or suit. Pants are appropriate, just be respectful with your choices. No low-cut blouses are acceptable here.

## BE ABLE TO TIE A TIE.

Some skills are just nice to have. Like being able to change a tire, bake a roast, speak another language, and . . . you guessed it, tie a tie. Although this skill is especially nice for men to acquire, you ladies would do well to learn, too. Someday you may find yourself either a) working in a restaurant or fashion business that requires you to wear (or tie) a tie, b) dating or befriending some unfortunate male who does not have the capability, c) raising some little males of your own who need your guidance, or d) marrying a movie star who's too busy signing autographs and writing checks for the needy to tie the bowtie on his tux for the Oscar's (hey, you might as well dream). Read on for both written instructions and how-to diagrams on tying neckties and bowties.

## HOW TO TIE A NECK TIE

Begin in front of a mirror. It will help you to see the length of your tie. Making sure your shirt is buttoned up completely, place your tie around your neck and under the collar of your shirt, with the wide end on the right (if you are left-handed, just switch the sides). Be sure to let the wide end hang twice as long as the narrow end. Here we go:

**1.** Holding the wide end over the narrow end, go behind the narrow end and through the loop at the center of the neck.

**2.** Take the wide end and wrap it around the narrow end toward the right side.

**3.** Take the wide end up to the center (in the front), and over the loop so that you see the back of the tie, and move it to the left side.

**4.** Bring the wide end back across to the right side (notice the knot forming).

**5.** Take the wide end from the back up through the neck loop.

**6.** Bring it through the loop that you just made in the front.

**7.** Straighten the knot so that it is in the center of your collar.

**8.** Be sure that your tie extends to the waist of your pants.

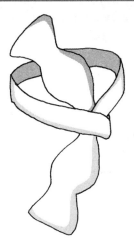

If this is your first time, try using a silk tie. They are much easier to tie. As you become better at tying your bow tie, you can try cotton ones.

**1.** Wrap the tie around your shirt collar.

**2.** Make sure one end is longer, maybe an inch or two, and take that end and cross the other.

**3.** Bring the long end up and come through the loop from the bottom.

**4.** Now fold the short end over itself in a bow shape.

**5.** Take the long end over the middle of the loop you just made.

**6.** Using your thumb that is holding the short end, push the center of the long end behind the short end and take it through the loop at the back of the bow tie.

**7.** Make adjustments to your bow tie by a little tugging here and there, and make sure the knot is in the center.

**I know all of you older people think you "have" to get dressed up, but that is just not my style. And looking around at other people and even the magazines, I'm not alone . . .**

Regardless of how casual the current style may be, know there are certain occasions (weddings, funerals, ceremonies, graduations, fancy dinners) that call for you to get dressed up. Just buck up and do it. No one will accuse you of going "meterosexual." And nothing says "youth and inexperience" like looking sloppy when the occasion calls for looking nice.

**What about tattoos?**

I could go on about how that little butterfly or screaming eagle that looks so cool at twenty-five might not have the same effect at age fifty-one, but you've heard it all before. So here's Mom's definitive rule about tattoos: don't get one when you are drinking. You might regret that decision forever. Tattoos may not always be a bad thing, but you want to be sober and alert if you make that decision.

**I'm a girl who prefers the natural look. Do I have to wear a lot of makeup to job interviews and special events?**

It's great to be who you are, but even if you aren't into much makeup, unless you have the complexion of a supermodel, you might consider wearing minimal makeup for special occasions. Nothing flashy, just be yourself—but don't look like you rolled out of bed. And always remember, a little lipstick or gloss brightens up your face and look considerably. Mom says don't leave home without it.

## Just one more thing . . .

❖**Even cool t-shirts have limits.** Save your concert t-shirts for the weekends. Unless you work in a music store, your boss won't care that you saw Coldplay live last Saturday night.

❖**Check your breath!** Always have good-smelling breath. Bad breath can break up more relationships than a bad attitude. Buy some gum and mints and keep them with you all the time. Pop a mint in your mouth just before you speak with someone close up.

❖**Keep some things private!** Please be aware of how high or low your shirt/pants fits when you bend and stretch and move. We don't want to see your underwear (even if you think that little thong is cute, girls) or the moon rising early. Have a little class.

.................................................

*"Fashion can be bought.*
*Style one must possess."*
**— EDNA WOOLMAN CHASE**

# CHAPTER NINE

# Relationships 101:
## Friends, Dates, & Roommates

*"Treat others the way you want to be treated."*
**— MATTHEW 7:12**

At the risk of sounding trite or even simplistic, I still have to say it: life is all about relationships. Think about it—each one of us has been in relationships of one kind or another since the day we were born.

Now that you are on your own, you are in the unique position to choose and enjoy relationships with no up-close guidance from Mom and Dad. To go forward, you must draw on the skills you've been taught from childhood, as well as relying on your "gut instincts" now and then.

The journey to seeking, finding, losing, and keeping lifelong relationships can be difficult at times, but it is always worth it. And if you are true to yourself along the way, you will have little to regret.

## First things first: Know what makes relationships succeed.

We are all unique, with different personalities and preferences. But whether we're shy or outgoing, cynical or idealistic, Pepsi or Coke fans, we all need relationships. Without them we would shrivel up inside. Though we may be drawn to different types of people and approach these precious bonds of life differently, Mom's learned through experience that successful relationships usually have several characteristics in common:

**Trust** – Trust is a confidence in the good will, loyalty, and integrity of another person. It doesn't happen overnight; that's why Mom often says to go slow. You need to spend time with another person, sharing experiences—both good and bad— to be able to develop trust and belief in someone. Once you do, however, having another person's trust is the most wonderful compliment you can ever be paid.

**Respect** – Respect is essentially placing *value* on other people and holding them in high regard. Although every human being deserves respect, in another way, respect is something that must be earned. To show respect is to honor another person. You can do this with your words, your tone of voice, and your actions. Show others respect and you will earn theirs.

**Common Interests** – Having common interests is easy to define: you like the same things. You can have respect for someone and even trust that person, but if you don't have anything in common, your relationship isn't going much further. Sharing experiences and enjoying the same types of hobbies and passions are crucial for a relationship to continue.

**Quality (and Quantity) Time Together** – As you get to know someone, more than likely you will know if you want the relationship to continue. If so, then you will want to spend more time with that person. Spending time together strengthens relationships.

**Two-Sided** – A relationship won't last for long if it is one-sided. Relationships are give-and-take. You can't always be the giver, because you will feel left out and exhausted. And, you can't always be the taker either because the other person in the relationship will grow tired of you and your selfishness fast.

**Communication** – Communication is key to any relationship, and the ability to communicate is crucial for a relationship to succeed. Remember, communicating isn't just about talking. It's also about listening, interpreting, and that loud-though-unspoken kind of "talk" called body language. Being able to succeed at any relationship will largely depend on your mastery of these skills.

Someone sent me an email once with a quote that I printed and saved. It made a lot of sense to me and really made me think deeply about my relationships with others. I don't know the author, but it is a wonderful example of how we all should think and act. It goes like this:

**The least important word: I**
**The most important word: We**
**The 2 most important words:**
Thank you.
**The 3 most important words:**
You are forgiven.
**The 4 most important words:**
What is your opinion?
**The 5 most important words:**
You did a good job.
**The 6 most important words:**
I want to understand you better.

### BE OPEN TO FRIENDSHIP.

Mom recommends making friends everywhere you go. Smile at total strangers, look them in the eye, and say hello. Strike up a conversation while standing next to someone in line at the movies, sitting by someone in an airport, or waiting to be seated in a restaurant. Make a point to speak to the person sitting alone in a coffee shop or to converse with the person you are paying at the deli. I'm not recommending that you have deep conversations with every person you encounter, but it is important that you see and treat each individual as a human being

and not just "the check-out lady." You never know who you will meet, what you will learn, or what you will have in common. Plus, it's just nice.

It's also good to be on the lookout for events and classes on subjects that interest you. Love to read? Join a book club. Sports fan? Sign up for a softball team or a fantasy football league. It may take a little nerve, but it's a great opportunity to meet people who have the same interests as you. Of course, some of the people you meet at the "(Fill in Your Preference) Club" will forever remain polite acquaintances. But then again, the best friend you've ever had could be just around the corner.

**MOM-*sense*:** Pick up some greeting cards to keep on hand. Choose a few birthday, get well, sympathy, and blank cards for those times when you'll need them, and then send them to loved ones throughout the year. On some days, there is nothing nicer than getting a caring or funny card in the mail.

### CHOOSE FRIENDS WHO ARE GOOD FOR (AND TO) YOU.

This little bit of advice should be obvious, but for some reason, we Moms have to remind you of it now and then: Hang around people who build you up and help you to be a better person.

If you realize that your friends are critical of everything and make you feel depressed, angry, and bad about yourself, then guess what? It is time for a change. Search out a more supportive and friendly group—people with a more positive outlook on life. Don't get stuck in a group of whiners who tend to bring everyone down, including you.

On the other hand, you don't want to be around a bunch of "yes men" either. A true friend likes you just as you are, but cares enough to nudge you and be honest when you're out of line or need to step up your game. (They also tell you when you have broccoli in your teeth!) When you can completely be yourself, and yet you're inspired to be better, you know you are in good company.

## A Friend . . .

✛ is not envious or jealous.

✛ loves you when others don't.

✛ offers help when you need it.

✛ stands beside you in the worst of times.

✛ tells you the truth when you need to hear it.

✛ will give you hope.

✛ will hold you accountable.

✛ gives you the benefit of the doubt.

✛ mourns with you when things go wrong.

✛ celebrates with you when things go right.

## BE A GOOD LISTENER. (DON'T TALK TOO MUCH!)

Have you ever known a really cool person whom you love spending time with, and when you tried to analyze what was so great about him or her, it hit you: he/she's a great listener. Some people just seem to have that gift—of really being present with you when you talk, and absorbing what you say. It makes you feel good, right?

Well, how about trying to become a good listener yourself? Seek out the ability to make the person who is speaking feel like he/she is the most important person in the room, or the world for that matter.

For those of us who tend more toward the gift of gab, or even for those who are too busy or distracted to sit and be still, learning to listen can be difficult. But think of all the benefits of truly "tuning in" to others. . .

### Five Benefits of Listening

◆ **Listening shows others respect**
When you give the person who's speaking your full attention, your focus on him/her is a compliment.

◆ **Listening boosts your knowledge**
If you listen to the entire story, you might just learn something you didn't know.

◆ **Listening strengthens relationships**
You will make more friends by being a good listener than you ever will by being a "big talker."

### ◆Listening establishes loyalty

If you don't listen to people, they will go find someone else who will listen, no matter what type of relationship you have. Everyone needs to know that they are being heard.

### ◆Listening teaches humility

During conversations, many of us are too busy focusing on ourselves and what impressive thing we're going to say next to really listen. Imagine caring more about understanding others than about being understood.

## How to be a Good Listener

\*Don't interrupt the person who is talking.

\*Look at the person who's talking—in the eye—as much as possible.

\*Don't answer your cell phone (or text-message!) or be distracted by other things.

\*Ask questions to show that you care and are interested, and to verify that you're "on the same page" as the speaker.

\*Make brief comments to show you are focused on what they're saying.

\*Don't give your opinion unless it is asked for.

## TAKE THE TIME TO REMEMBER NAMES.

Guess what every person's favorite word is: *their name.* Think about it—haven't you ever been pleasantly surprised, even honored, when someone "important" or unexpected knows your name?

Calling you by name is like a small acknowledgement of your value as an individual. Try to give others that same little verbal salute. This habit will also help you in social and business situations.

## Tips for Remembering Names

✓Pay close attention when you are introduced. Repeat the name a couple of times during the course of the conversation. (Don't be too obvious.)

✓Ask for the spelling of an unusual or difficult name. This will help you remember it later.

✓Try to connect the name with another common rhyming word, like "Stan the Man," or "Valerie at the Gallery."

✓Find out the person's occupation or a hobby and visualize him/her in that capacity.

✓Write down the name soon after meeting the person.

## IF YOU CAN'T SAY ANYTHING NICE, DON'T SAY ANYTHING AT ALL.

How many times did your Mom suggest this guiding principle to you? Well, my mother and grandmother told me it over and over again. I just wish I'd followed it more often! It is so much easier to complain, criticize, and whine when things aren't going the way you want. But inevitably, after a little rant about some person or situation, you end up regretting your words or hurting someone. Life is hard enough without piling on the burden of negative words.

There is good to be found in everyone and everything. Take the time to look a little deeper. In fact, why not challenge yourself to avoid complaining altogether? Why not refuse to talk about others? A few times in my life, at someone's funeral, I've heard a person described—in tones of awe—with these words: "I can't remember hearing him/her ever talk badly about anyone." What a tribute to that person! What a gracious life!

If you find negativity is the norm for conversation in work or social settings, don't jump on the bandwagon. Rack your brain for something constructive to say. And if you can't—or don't want to—say something nice, then take Mom's advice. Don't say anything at all. Sometimes, having good manners is as much about what you *don't* say as what you do.

## SEE THE VALUE IN EVERYONE.

Remember that old saying, "Don't judge a man unless you've walked a mile in his shoes"? Well, the same caution applies to judging girls in three-inch-heels. If there is one thing that Mom hopes you remember, it is this: *Everyone has value*. Each person has something about him or her that is unique. Each person has a story, one that could make you cry if you knew it, or at least let you see that person differently. Everyone wants and needs to be accepted by others.

In our fast-paced world, we don't take the time to look past differences and see the human beneath the stereotype, first impression, or annoying habit. It is just too easy to keep going about our own business and to think that we don't need to interact with people who are different or difficult. Believe it or not, we humans are more alike than we are different. Give people the benefit of the doubt. You can never have too many friends. And you may just find one in the last place you'd look.

## Key Points to Finding Value in Others

★Be realistic in your expectations of others.

★Try your best not to compare and compete with others.

★Find one common thing that you and another person share.

★Focus on the strengths of a person.

★View that person with the same compassion you'd want people to show you on your worst day.

★Look past the outer shell and see what is on the inside.

★Remember that everyone has a story.

## DATING: REMEMBER THE POSSIBILITIES.

Although physical attraction and the longing for companionship go back to Adam and Eve, the practice of dating is relatively modern. And boy has it changed since the days we Moms wore corsages to the prom! With online dating, speed dating, and personal ads, dating has jumped headfirst into the 21st century. But even though all these new dating schemes are out there, it still comes down to this: two people who spend time together and get to know each other.

Dating is not an exact science. The process involves a little planning, some research, and time for development. It sounds a little like business, huh? Well not quite. Dating is more about possibilities. You might have a great time. You might fall in love. You might be bored to tears or get your heart broken. Mom recommends that you approach dating with an open mind, high hopes, and no expectations. (The "no expectations" is the hard part—especially if your brain is filled with famous lines from romantic movies and novels!)

How do you find good people to date? The same way you find out about everything else, like jobs, restaurants, and places to live. You date people you meet through your family and friends. Your friends are probably your best bet in this department. Of course, your Mom is always standing by with her perfect idea of a partner for you. Wink, wink.

## BE CREATIVE WHEN DATING.

Believe it or not, Mom knows that dates today don't always mean dinner and a movie. (Not like in the olden times.) There are many other outlets that will provide opportunities to talk and allow you to get to know a person better. I'm sure you have plenty of ideas in this department, but just in case, read on for some of mine.

### Ideas for Dates (You don't have to give me the credit!)

- ❖ Browse at a bookstore
- ❖ Take a walk
- ❖ Have a picnic in a park
- ❖ Go to a carnival or fair
- ❖ Catch a concert
- ❖ Play miniature golf
- ❖ Attend a play
- ❖ Watch a sporting event
- ❖ Visit a gallery opening or museum

## KNOW WHO'S GETTING THE BILL.

Back in the good old days when Mom and Dad dated, Dad paid for everything. Things are a little different today. Guys don't always pay for everything. The rule of thumb is, *whoever did the inviting also does the paying.* Assume that the inviter is paying, unless it is

So you've made plans and the date day is here. Here are a few guidelines to make sure that the date will at least be pleasant:

✴ **Be on time.** *Don't make someone wait too long for you. It's just not nice.*

✴ **Dress for the occasion.** *Ask where you're going, and don't overdo it or under-do it.*

✴ **Be interested in the other person** *and participate in the conversation.*

✴ **Relax and enjoy the date, even if you will never go out again.** *You can have a pleasant time without sparks.*

✴ **Easy does it on the drinking.** *Nothing is worse than a date that is drunk, and you'll want your wits about you!*

---

talked about before. If the "who's paying" issue feels unsettled and you plan to pay, mention it at the start of the date: "Hey this night is on me, okay?" This will put you both at ease and help you have a relaxing date.

Of course, there are exceptions to every rule, so be prepared. Have some cash or a credit card with you no matter what. Another option is to plan to go Dutch and have each person pay his or her own way. It would be smart to work this out before the check comes: "Dinner would be fantastic—how about going Dutch on the bill?" One other choice is to split the parts of the date: "Thanks for inviting me to the play, can I get dinner afterward?" Knowing up-front can make the night more enjoyable.

**BE A GRATEFUL DATE.**

At the end of the date, no matter if you had a good time or not, thank your date for the nice time you spent together. It is a simple, kind, and appropriate gesture to be thankful and grateful to someone when they have spent time and/or money on you.

It is also appropriate to call the next day and talk to the person or leave a message saying what a good time you had. Only do this if you want to see that person again. It could send the wrong message if you don't.

If you had the best time of your life and you think you have met your soul mate (really, on one date?), send the person a short, handwritten note. Don't go overboard, but be appropriate in your thanks. If it really is your soul mate, then you will have gotten off on the right foot. Good luck!

## SHOW MATURITY WITH YOUR CELL PHONE (THE RELATIONSHIP CONNECTOR).

Ah, the cell phone, the device no one can live without. Well, believe it or not, Mom remembers life before the cell phone. And guess what? We still talked to our friends, we still made plans and arrived at our destinations, and when we were away from our house and needed to call, we put a dime in an antique called a "pay-phone!" I know it is a little hard to believe. Now even Mom depends on that mobile ringer.

While a cell phone is a wonderful tool to have in case of an emergency, it can frankly be the biggest pain in the butt ever. Its "crimes" are many—going off at a movie, play, or, heaven forbid, in church or at a wedding; forcing others to endure loud, trivial conversations at restaurants or in the grocery line; causing drivers to barely avoid smashing your car while they laugh and talk with a friend. Oh, I get irritated just thinking about it.

So, forgive my intrusion into your personal technology, but I would be failing my Mom-ly duty if I didn't share a few "cell phone rules" with you.

## Cell Phone Etiquette

✗ **Turn the phone to silent, vibrate, or off when you are in a meeting, movie, concert, church, or library.** (Many other places can be added to this list.)

✗ **Don't use your cell phone for private conversations in front of other people.** It makes others uncomfortable, and do you really want everyone to know the mundane details of your life? Call the person back later.

✗ **Walk outside to make or take a call.** It is more polite to excuse yourself, if the call is urgent, than to offend and disturb other people.

✗ **Practice restraint when text messaging around other people.** It is very distracting and dare I say, rude, since it proves that your full attention is not really where you are, but somewhere else instead.

✗ **Turn the volume down.** The loud volume on cell phones is very annoying. I don't need to hear your favorite song in the check-out line at Target.

✗ **Don't use your cell phone headset in public.** In addition to looking like you work for the Secret Service, you will talk louder than you imagine, and trust Mom, it's just plain annoying.

## ROOMMATES: HANDLE WITH CARE.

You are ready to live on your own, be an adult, take control of your life, and be responsible. But there is one small problem: you can't afford to live by yourself. So, you've got to find a roommate. Scientists may disagree, but Moms know that having a roommate is one of the biggest human experiments in history. It can be wonderful, challenging, fabulous, stressful, fun, and/or miserable, and that's just the first week. Let's just hope for your benefit that you have the greatest roommate on the face of the earth. It has happened, you know—some people are lifelong friends because they once were roommates. And then there's the flip side of that, where former best friends don't ever speak again after sharing a refrigerator together. Being an inexact science, it's hard to predict . . .

Regardless of who you live with, at the very minimum, **roommates should be able to:**

✔**co-exist** peacefully,

✔**commit** to a short-term lease,

✔**communicate** openly & honestly,

✔**compromise** on sticky subjects,

✔**cooperate** on split expenses for keeping up the house, and

✔**be considerate** of each other's time, space, and possessions.

## BE CHOOSY.

Having heard my share of roommate disasters, here's Mom's advice: be choosy when selecting or agreeing to be a roommate. Don't live with your best friend, and don't live with an absolute stranger. Live with someone that you have a connection with and whose values and lifestyle seem similar to yours, rather than someone you are extremely close to. (Living with your best friend opens up the possibility that your friendship could be irreversibly damaged because one of you never takes out the garbage.) Often when you live with people, you start to see their little irritating habits—we all have them—and it can be hard to get past that.

### Questions To Ask When Finding a Roommate

★ **Do you smoke?**
★ **Do you mind that I smoke?**
★ **Will anyone be allowed to smoke in our house?**

*Best Decision:*
No smoking inside.

**Do you mind splitting up the household chores?** No compromises here, 50/50 split—or else resentment will kick in fast.

**Do you have any pets?** Make sure that dogs will be walked often, cat hair will be vacuumed up, and that litter boxes, hamster cages, and fish tanks will be cleaned often. No loud pets. *(Blame this rule on the neighbors.)*

**Where do you work? Are you a student?** Beware of unemployed or sketchy answers concerning work. Student's schedules can be way different from someone who works—make sure that's okay in advance.

**Are you a night owl?** Since everyone doesn't have the same schedule, conflicts often pop up here.

**Are you a big drinker? Do any drugs?** It is okay to ask this—better to know in advance.

**Are you dating anyone?** You should agree up-front what the rules are for overnight guests.

**Will you have many out-of-town visitors?** Make the rules clear about possible company camping out on your living room floor.

**What has been your biggest complaint about former roommates?** An answer here might just stop the deal.

**Do you have a set budget?** You could wind up paying for more than your fair share if your roommate can't afford household necessities.

**Do you watch a lot of TV, and what kind of music do you like?** Issues can often arise over these subjects.

**Can I get references from former landlords?** It would be good to know if your potential roommate pays bills on time and follows the rules.

**Do you throw parties often?** If so, you need to be aware that your stuff could be damaged if things get out of control, or the police could show up for a visit.

If you detect that the "potential" roommate is uncomfortable with any of the questions or doesn't seem to be completely honest, you might want to pass and try the next one. It may take a few tries before you settle on the person you think will work.

## SET SOME HOUSE RULES.

You've settled on a roommate, now what? First things first: develop a set of house rules that both of you (or all of you, if there's more than two) agree on. Each person should make a list of their thoughts on the subject of by-laws, and then you should get together and combine them. Post the rules in an inconspicuous place like inside your pantry door where each of you can be reminded.

+ **The kitchen sink** – Everyone do your own dishes every time you use them.
+ **Bathroom** – Clean your own if you have it, otherwise alternate weeks to clean it.
+ **Kitchen** – Clean it as you go, and leave no crumb trail.
+ **Food** – Eat your own unless you shop and cook (and pay) together, and then share responsibly.
+ **Living room/den** – Clean up after yourself and don't leave anything behind.
+ **TV** – First come, first served, with a two-hour limit, or length of a movie or ballgame.
+ **Noise** – Show consideration here for sleep, study, work, or movies.
+ **Other people's things** – Never borrow unless you ask, and then return clean promptly.

## ADDRESS PROBLEMS CALMLY AND QUICKLY.

Your roommate didn't pay the electric bill, *or* had friends over again that trashed the kitchen and living room, *or* borrowed your favorite shirt and got ketchup all over it. You are angry, and the "stuff" has hit the proverbial fan. What now?

Hopefully, having a talk while you both are calm and collected will lead to a compromise and a settlement. Give your living arrangement some time; remember that trying to bring two (or more) different people with different lifestyles and backgrounds together under the same roof can be difficult at times. It is essential for each

## HOW TO SETTLE A ROOMMATE DISPUTE

1. Have a cooling down time for a day or two.
2. Don't let the problem get worse by waiting too long.
3. Have a solution ready when you do talk.
4. Choose a good time to talk, and do it rationally and respectfully.
5. Revisit the rules you made together.

person to be comfortable with the house rules and with everyone's effort toward making the living situation work well.

Finally, if it doesn't work out and the strain is rough on each of you, try to "end it" as peacefully as possible. Making sure that each party pays their fair share of the agreed-upon expenses, move on (or out), and dream of the day when you will marry and live with your dream roommate in perfect harmony, with no problems adjusting whatsoever.

**MOM-*sense*:** Don't expect your roommate to be an extension of your family. His or her own family may be very different from yours and just might have a different image of what home or family is.

### LAST, BUT CERTAINLY NOT LEAST: KINDNESS COUNTS.

Do you remember being reminded by your Mom to say *please* and *thank you*? That's because she wanted you to grow up to be respectful and polite. Along your journey, I hope you've realized that being kind to other people includes more than just saying please or thank you, even though those words are a great place to start.

Try being kind to everyone you see, not just the people you know. (But especially to the people you do know—sometimes we treat strangers better than we do those closest to us!) Say hello to people. Ask how people are doing. Open a door for someone. Help carry a heavy package. Do something for a family member or a friend without being asked. Take a little time to really focus on being kind. You will never know what your kindness may mean to someone. Plus it might just rub off on someone else.

## J.A.M. Session: Just one more thing . . .

☆ **Mind your own business.** It really is as simple as that. It is hard enough to keep up with things in your own life.

☆ **Always respond to people.** If someone tries to contact you in any form—by mail, telephone, email, or whatever—respond. It is rude to ignore them. Adults do not blow people off.

☆ **Remember the song you learned as a kid:**

*Make new friends,*
*But keep the old*
*One is silver,*
*And the other gold.*

# CHAPTER TEN

# Safety First

*"It's better to be safe than sorry."*

A s you go through the hustle and bustle of your daily work (and play) day, safety may not be your first priority. Too often, it is easy to think we're invincible, that standard precautions (and speed limits) don't apply to us, and that—unless we're a S.W.A.T. team member, stunt double, or race car driver—dangerous situations always happen to other people.

The truth is, no matter who you are or where you live, safety should be considered in most every aspect of your life. That's why Mom is here to think about safety for you. Of course, Mom doesn't want you to be afraid or paranoid. But it never hurts to take a few precautions to make sure you stay safe.

## First things first: Live by basic safety rules.

As I said, in this day and age, safety is something we all must consider. The days of open windows and unlocked doors have disappeared with yesterday's premier of *The Andy Griffith Show*. Even if you live in Mayberry, be sure and follow these basic rules for safety:

**Be aware of your surroundings:** Look around and know what is going on. Be aware of people and buildings and cars. It only takes a second to glance in every direction to make sure you are safe.

**Don't walk alone:** Mom says there is safety in numbers. It is never a good idea to go somewhere that is isolated if you are alone, especially at night. Besides, friends are great to walk with and talk to; great conversations and ideas happen during walks.

**Be careful at the ATM:** Be quick, be careful, and be safe. Don't stand around counting your money or going through every step and transaction at the ATM. Get your money and go, and beware of the next customer in line looking over your back. When in your car, go to the ATM during the daylight hours.

**For your cell phone, remember ICE (In Case of Emergency):** Someone passed along this clever reminder to me, and I want to share it with you. Take out your cell phone right now and scroll to your closest family members' and friends' numbers, adding the letters ICE in front of that person's name. This will ensure that if something unforeseen happens to you and you need help, your cell phone can give your rescuer clues to find out who you are and how to help you. It is a very simple and smart thing to do.

**MOM-*sense*:** When going somewhere new, always write down or print out the directions. You just *think* you can remember everything. Write it down—you'll be glad you did.

## Keep your home secure.

Just because you are inside your apartment or house doesn't mean you should let your guard down. Take these few precautions to make your home feel safe and secure.

**Always lock your doors:** This is so simple that sometimes it gets overlooked. Lock those doors every single time you go in and out. If you have a chain lock or an extra deadbolt lock, use them too.

**Have outside lights that actually work:** Be sure your light fixture outside your door works and has good light bulbs in it at all times.

**Don't open the door to someone you don't know:** Mom is adamant about this one. Look through that peephole, and if that face isn't familiar, don't open it. (If you don't have a peephole, a drill and a peephole kit can fix that!)

**Keep a phone handy:** In these great days of cell phones, many homes no longer have landline phones. If you do have a landline phone, make sure you have one by your bed and another one in your kitchen or living room. If you are a cell phone user only, keep it with you all the time.

**Keep something in your home that can be used as a weapon:**
I'm not suggesting that you go out and buy a gun. A baseball bat makes an excellent weapon and can hurt someone besides the opposing pitcher if you need it to.

## KEEP YOUR AUTOMOBILE SAFE AND RUNNING WELL.

Car and automobile safety are often disregarded because, once again, most people think *it can never happen to me.* Well, it *can* happen to you, so be prepared. The first rule in auto safety is to make sure you have a good running and reliable vehicle. In order for your vehicle to be reliable, you should maintain it and take good care of it.

**Have your oil checked regularly:**
No, it's not "optional"; you should have your oil changed between every 2,000 and 3,000 miles. Keeping your oil changed will help your engine and your wallet. Find a good oil-change business or an auto dealer and stop in for regular check-ups. During the inspection, they will also check your oil filter, air filter, hoses, battery, tire pressure, etc.

**Maintain your tires:** Driving day in and day out can be tough on your tires, so regularly check to make sure they are properly inflated. (Most oil change businesses will do this for you.)

You should also watch your tires for wear and tear. The treads can wear down if you are driving, and this can be unsafe, especially in rainy or bad weather. (Worn-out treads don't have the best traction.)

MOM-*sense*: To make sure your tire treads are still holding their own, do the "Penny Test." Take an ordinary U.S. penny and insert it between the treads of your tire, making sure that Abraham Lincoln's head goes in first. If you can see any part of Abe's head, then you need to consider buying new tires.

## HOW TO BE A DEFENSIVE DRIVER

✓ Drive at a reasonable, safe speed.

✓ Keep your eyes on the road, not the i-Pod or the cell phone text messages.

✓ Watch the cars around you and what they are doing.

✓ Keep your hands on the wheel; you can eat later.

✓ Read the road signs.

✓ Don't drive too closely behind someone else.

✓ Use your blinkers, let other drivers know you are turning.

✓ Use your horn if you need to; it's there for a reason.

✓ If someone cuts you off or commits another road foul, try to restrain your temper.

### Remember this:

**1.** More than likely, you've committed a traffic faux pas once in your life (accidentally, of course).

**2.** The other driver may be an idiot, a jerk, or both, and you may be entirely justified in your indignation, but you don't want to start a confrontation—you can be 100% right and still end up maimed, or worse. Just practice your patience and self-control; it's good for you.

**3.** That idiot driver is likely somebody's granddaddy, son, pregnant wife, or a Mom with a car full of screaming kids.

It is also a really good idea to rotate your tires about every 6,000 miles. Rotating tires assures that your tires will wear at the same rate. Remember to keep a watch on those tires and take care of them because they are your car's guardians on the road!

**Make repairs A.S.A.P.:** If you have anything wrong with your automobile, make every effort to have it repaired just as soon as you can. Brakes that screech, lights that flicker, or thing-a-ma-jiggy's that hang loose can eventually cause an accident.

**Lock your doors:** No matter where you are or how safe you think the area is, you should always, always, *always lock your doors*. We all keep so many things in our cars these days, and folks who don't take Mom's advice to lock up can be easy targets.

**Have your keys in your hand and ready:** When you are heading to your car, be sure to have your keys in your hand and ready to either unlock your door or stick into the ignition. Having your keys handy and ready eliminates the time it would take you to dig in your pocket or purse to find them.

Before you get back into your car after you have been out of it for any time, you should always give it a once-over with your eyes to make sure that things look all right. Take a Moment to glance at your tires, windows, and doors. And don't forget to look in the backseat before you get inside.

**Organize your glove compartment:** There are a few basic items that need to take permanent residence in your glove compartment. They should be organized and accessible.

- Vehicle registration form
- Proof of insurance
- Card with emergency contacts
- Flashlight & batteries
- *For ladies,* mace or pepper spray

**Wear your seatbelt religiously:** Don't even start your car without your seatbelt clicked into place. It can save your life. Mom knows about this because it saved hers!

**Be a defensive driver:** Driving these days can often be a real headache. Traffic is heavy, people are angry or distracted, and you often spend more time in the car than planned. Be ready for anything when you go out in your car, and pay attention. And please don't drive too fast like some maniac or Indy racer; you are neither.

**Don't drive like a maniac in bad weather:** Okay, use that brain in your head there. Slow down when it is raining, sleeting, or snowing. Remember that wet stuff falling out of the sky is landing on the roads and will be slick. You need to get where you are going alive and in one piece.

**Never drink or do drugs and drive:** This may sound like a very common-sense piece of advice, and it is. However, you would be surprised how many knuckle-headed people get behind the wheel every single day while intoxicated or under the influence of drugs. The consequences of such reckless behavior could be life-changing (and ending) for you and someone in your path. It isn't worth it.

Consider what you would do if you hit a family in another car and killed them. Consider what your family would do if you ran off the road and were severely injured or even killed. Think before you participate in any behavior that will impair your judgment. If there is a possibility you may be in a questionable state of coherence, make plans for getting home safely that doesn't include you driving.

**Have an extra key somewhere:** It is a great idea to have a good friend or family member keep a spare key to your vehicle. You might just lock yourself out one day (believe me, it happens) and this could be what saves you from spending one hundred dollars or more on a locksmith. Also, think about keeping a spare inside your wallet.

## FOLLOW BIKE SAFETY.

Riding a bike is a great way to get exercise, help the environment, and save the money you would have spent on expensive gasoline or other transportation bucks. Bikes need to be cared for just like your automobile. If you use your bike often, maintain it and make sure all parts are working properly.

**Buy the correct size of bike:** Don't just buy what looks good or the bike with a brand name you recognize. Try them on for size and ask for help to ensure you get a good fit.

**Keep tires inflated:** Make sure your tires are inflated before you take off on your bike. You could be walking soon if you don't.

**Check your chains:** Lubricate your chains and check them for wear, rust, and correct placement.

**Have reflectors on your bike:** Reflectors are an important feature that will protect you in traffic. Make sure your reflectors are in the right places to be seen.

**Wear your helmet:** Just like wearing a seatbelt in a car, you should not ride without a helmet. It, too, can save your life. (And you look so cool wearing it!)

**Keep identification on you:** Never ride without identification on you.

## BE VIGILANT ON WALKS OR RUNS.

Hooray for you; you're exercising! But let's be smart while doing so. Mom would prefer that you walk or run with a friend or partner. Since that isn't always convenient or even an option, please follow these precautions before pounding the pavement:

- Always tell someone when you leave and where you are going.
- Keep identification on you.
- Carry a cell phone.
- Use well traveled paths.
- At night, stay in lighted areas.
- Dress appropriately in cold and hot weather.
- Make sure you are hydrated before you go.
- Let the same person know when you return.

## BE PREPARED FOR EMERGENCIES.

We never know when an emergency will strike. Whether it be weather like floods, tornados, or blizzards; fire; or someone breaking in your home, you should be prepared. No one likes to be caught off-guard, so take a few Moments now to ensure that you are equipped to handle an emergency situation.

No matter the situation, it is a great idea to have bottled water on hand and some canned foods and dry, non-perishable food. Especially in bad weather situations, you need to have food and water that could last you a couple of days, if the need exists. You can live on dry cereal if you must.

### Weather Emergencies

1. Keep the television on to listen for weather updates.
2. Have a battery-powered radio on hand.
3. Have your cell phone charged and on you.
4. Be prepared to leave if conditions worsen.
5. Have a route planned for leaving.
6. Make sure you have food and appropriate clothes in your car or in a bag.
7. Be sure to have a safe place if you live in a tornado area.
8. Take weather warnings seriously and don't be irresponsible.

### Fire Emergencies

1. Have smoke detectors in your home and check them once a month.
2. Be sure to have an escape route if your home is on fire.
3. Have a small fire-proof safe to keep valuable papers inside.
4. Never leave candles burning when you are not around.
5. Never go into a room that is on fire.
6. If you can't escape, place towels or blankets around door openings, get down low and cover your mouth and nose to prevent smoke inhalation.
7. Call 911 immediately.

### Break-Ins

1. When entering your home, always be aware of everything around you.
2. Make sure no one is behind you when you enter.
3. If your door isn't locked as it should be, don't go inside.
4. Immediately, get away from there and call 911.
5. Remember, you may not be equipped to handle a really dangerous situation.
6. If you are trapped by an intruder, stay as calm as possible.
7. Look around for ways to defend yourself or to alert someone you need help.

Here are some quotes I've accumulated for you to remind you
to make safety a priority:

*Prepare and prevent, don't repair and repent.*
— **AUTHOR UNKNOWN**

*Safety is as simple as ABC—Always Be Careful.*
— **AUTHOR UNKNOWN**

*Safety doesn't happen by accident.*
— **AUTHOR UNKNOWN**

*Better a thousand times careful than once dead.*
— **PROVERB**

*Safety First is Safety Always*
— **CHARLES M. HAYES**

*Safety is a cheap and effective insurance policy.*
— **EDWARD COKE**

*The safest risk is the one you didn't take.*
— **AUTHOR UNKNOWN**

*Safety isn't expensive, it's priceless.*
— **AUTHOR UNKNOWN**

# CHAPTER ELEVEN

# Very Basic First Aid, Common Remedies, & Good Health

*"An apple a day keeps the doctor away."*

Most Moms have no degree in medicine (okay, some do), nor are they nurses (okay, some are), but they can pretty much handle most situations that happen at home. They might get queasy at the sight of blood or maybe just grossed out, but Moms everywhere know that the key is not to panic. You, too, can handle the minor "at home" accidents if you keep your head. And if the situation gets too serious, there's always 911.

Very basic first aid is what Mom wants you to know. For more serious accidents, like severe burns, head injures, deep cuts, or possible broken bones, please seek medical attention quickly. You should also get help if you have stabbing pain anywhere, or high fevers over 100 degrees that are lingering after a day. The tips Mom's sharing here are exactly that: tips for minor cuts, bumps, bruises, aches, and pains. These are jobs that the average person (yes, that means you!) can take care of without seeking medical help from professionals.

**Note:** This section/chapter is only an informational guide. These are only the opinions of the author. The practices discussed here in no way suggest that medical attention from professionals should be avoided. The author and CPO Publishing assume no responsibility for the use or administration for any of the first aid practices discussed.

## First things first: Pack a first-aid kit.

In most large discount stores, drug stores, and even grocery stores today you can find pre-packaged first-aid kits. Usually, these have one brand of everything a company makes, and you might only use three items in the box. This Mom prefers to pack her own and buy things that she really will use.

First of all, you need to pick out a good, easy-to-find spot for your kit. My suggestion? Either your kitchen or bathroom. Mom keeps hers in the kitchen because that seems to be where things always happen—or at least the first place people run to ask for help. An accessible drawer or cabinet is the best spot. With this helpful assortment on-hand, you'll be more prepared than a boy scout.

**MOM-*sense*:** While you're getting all prepared for life's emergencies, consider taking a first-aid and CPR course at your college or local community center. You will learn valuable basic skills that will give you confidence in emergency situations and perhaps save someone's life someday.

### INCLUDE THESE ITEMS IN YOUR FIRST-AID KIT:

✓Basket or box to hold the items
✓Digital therMometer
✓Antacid/gas relief
✓Antihistamine
✓Antibiotic ointment
✓Band-Aid-type adhesive bandages
✓Gauze or bandage squares
✓Bandage tape
✓Diarrhea medication
✓Bottle of pain relief, i.e. aspirin, acetaminophen, etc.
✓Hydrogen peroxide
✓Calamine lotion
✓Elastic bandage
✓Hot water bottle
✓Ice pack (instant or one that can be filled with ice)
✓Tweezers
✓Burn ointment

### KNOW HOW TO ALLEVIATE COMMON AILMENTS AND ILLNESSES.

Let's face it, sooner or later, you will contract a virus from someone or come down with another ailment. Even with flu shots, chicken noodle soup, and vitamin C, it is inevitable—one day when you least expect it, you will have a runny nose, or a rash, or a yucky cough. Mom wishes she could always be there to take care of you, but since she can't, here's a basic primer to get you through.

## The plain, old, common cold

Unfortunately, medical science has never found a cure for the common cold. (Mom doesn't like to criticize, but come on, what's the holdup, guys?) Once in an inconvenient while, you'll probably get all the symptoms: runny nose, stuffy head, sore throat, and maybe a little fever and some aches. You know the drill—drink lots of liquids, take vitamin C, get some rest, and let it run its course. (Also, you could try some of Mom's chicken soup from the recipes chapter. It really does work wonders and is not difficult to make. Check out the recipe on page 105.

Several of today's over-the-counter medications are geared toward specific symptoms. If what you think is a cold seems to hang on and on, you may need to see your doctor in case it's a bacterial sinus infection or a case of strep throat.

## Constipation

Okay, so your tummy hurts and it's been a while since you've gone to the bathroom. Remember that you need to have a bowel movement every day. Try drinking lots of water and eat some food that is high in fiber. (Remember the apple-a-day line? Well those apples and their skin are good sources of fiber.) A mild laxative could do the trick if foods don't.

## Diarrhea

Now we are at the complete opposite of the aforementioned ailment. If you are suffering from diarrhea, stay away from spicy foods and milk. Drink a good amount of liquids so you won't get dehydrated. You can also try an anti-diarrhea medicine if it lasts longer than a half a day. If you continue to suffer from diarrhea even with the medication, please contact your doctor.

## Flu *(Short for Influenza)*

If you've got the flu, you'll know it by the body aches. The flu can also make you feel exhausted, give you fever, sore throat, coughing, and even make you nauseous. Mom's best advice for the flu is rest, rest, and more rest. Drink a lot of fluids, eat a lot of soup and Jello, and sleep a great deal. Hopefully, it won't last more than a few days.

## Headaches

Headaches are a pain in the . . . head. Actually, headaches can be quite debilitating. So, don't leave your headache untreated and be miserable. Over-the-counter pain relievers can help with headaches. If they become unbearable, see a doctor.

## Migraines

Migraines are chronic headaches that can cause dizziness and blurred vision. They usually occur in the same area of your head. You should see a doctor if you suspect you have a migraine headache, because there are great medications for them.

## Stress/Tension

With these headaches, you can also have pain in your neck and shoulders. Try relaxing and stretching to help in addition to medication.

## Sinus

Sinus headaches are usually a symptom of sinusitis. With these headaches, you can have facial pain especially above and underneath your eyes. Try a sinus headache medication.

## Rashes

A rash can appear on your skin just about anywhere and could be caused by any variety of reasons. If you do have some mysterious rash that is painful, red, and spreading, you should see a doctor. You could possibly have gotten an insect bite that could be dangerous.

## Hives

Hives are typically allergic reactions that can cause your skin to itch, swell, and become very red. The rash can cover a large or small area. Hives can be caused by food allergies, medication allergies, or insect bites. For mild cases of hives, you should take an antihistamine, and perhaps take an oatmeal bath. For more severe cases, see your doctor.

## Eczema

Eczema is a common skin condition that can leave you with red, dry, irritated, itchy patches. Normally you would see a doctor to be diagnosed with eczema. A doctor will often prescribe creams and ointments to soothe and eliminate the irritation and redness. Don't scratch, don't stay in water too long, stay cool, avoid stress, and use Vaseline petroleum jelly to moisturize the cracks in your skin.

## Urinary tract infections

These infections can happen to men or women and can be very painful. A urinary tract infection can involve your kidneys, bladder, or other parts of your urinary tract. Symptoms can include frequent urination that burns, possible fever, and feeling just plain tired. These infections are caused by bacteria, so you will likely need to see a doctor to have antibiotic medications prescribed for you.

### KNOW ABOUT SERIOUS AND CHRONIC ILLNESSES.

While all of us must suffer through minor bouts with sickness now and then, some of us have more serious ongoing conditions to confront. The good news is, today's modern medicines can help treat many of these illnesses and make living with them easier.

## Asthma

Asthma is an illness that involves the respiratory system. During an attack, sufferers can struggle to breathe when the airway is narrowed. Asthma attacks can be triggered by exertion or exercise; warm, cold, or moist air; and stress. For proper diagnosis and medications, you should see a doctor if you suspect asthma or if you are having any breathing problems.

## Depression

Depression is much more than just feeling blue or down in the dumps. It can be caused by psychological, genetic, or even environmental factors. Symptoms of depression can be a lack or loss of interest in daily activities, repeated feelings of sadness, crying, changes in sleeping and eating patterns, not being able to concentrate, low self-esteem, and thoughts of death. Please seek medical help through your doctor if you are experiencing any of these symptoms. Treatment for depression often includes medication and/ or therapy.

## Diabetes

We all need insulin to convert sugar and starches into energy; diabetes is a disease that is caused by your body's inability to produce or use insulin properly. Symptoms of diabetes can be extreme hunger and thirst, frequent urination, weight loss, blurred vision, fatigue, and wounds that will not heal. Diabetes can be treated with medication, diet, and exercise. You should see a doctor if you suspect you have diabetes.

## Cancer

Cancer is a very complicated disease that doesn't discriminate and has over one hundred different types. There are a few symptoms that are commonly shared by most patients: fatigue, fever, skin changes, pain, and weight loss. Since cancer survival rates are greatly improved if diagnosed early, see your doctor if you have a combination of these symptoms over a period of time. Above all, remember that cancer prevention is so important and should be practiced by everyone. A few general rules for prevention are to eat lots of fruits and vegetables, don't smoke, wear sunscreen, don't eat too many meats with high animal fat content, avoid working closely with chemicals, exercise, practice safe sex, and know your family history.

## Gastro-intestinal problems

There are many different digestive disorders, and symptoms often vary depending on the particular problem. Make a doctor's appointment if you have changes in your bowel habits, blood in your stool, heartburn, weight loss, or severe abdominal pain. Treatments vary as well, but they can absolutely make a difference in your daily life.

## Mononucleosis

Perhaps better known as the "kissing disease," mononucleosis is most commonly seen in younger adults and teenagers. Mono is spread by saliva, usually by kissing, sharing a drink, or sharing eating utensils. Symptoms of mono often include fever, sore throats, swollen and tender lymph nodes, and extreme fatigue. You should see a doctor if you have these symptoms because mono can cause your spleen to swell and even burst. Don't take aspirin for the pain; use acetaminophen instead. Rest is a huge part of the recovery process of mono.

## Pneumonia

Pneumonia is an infection in your lungs that can cause a terrible cough, fever, chest pain, shortness of breath, headaches, and fatigue. You should see your doctor if you are wheezing or experiencing any of these symptoms. Most likely they will give you a chest X-ray, prescribe medicines, and let you recover at home, where you should get plenty of rest.

## Shingles

If you ever had chickenpox, you are a candidate for shingles. Shingles is a skin rash caused by the same virus as chickenpox, a virus that has remained dormant in your nerve tissues since your original illness. Shingles can be very painful and can leave annoying blisters on your skin, just like chickenpox. Unfortunately, shingles can last three to four weeks. If you suspect you may have shingles, see a doctor, who will probably treat you with medication and ointments. Be careful not to scratch the blisters! (You can spread chickenpox to someone who has never had it, but you cannot spread shingles to a former chickenpox patient.)

## Strep Throat

Strep throat is an infection that is caused by bacteria. Symptoms of strep throat are a sore throat, stomach pain, and red, swollen tonsils. Strep throat will need to be treated with antibiotics, so a visit to the doctor is required. Once again, you will need to get some rest if you are diagnosed.

## Toxic Shock Syndrome

Toxic shock is not a common illness, but it is bacterial in nature. Toxic shock is often associated with tampon use by women, but it can affect anyone who has any kind of staph infection. Toxic shock syndrome symptoms are very high fever, watery diarrhea, muscle aches, and headaches. You should see a doctor soon. Prevention of this illness, and staph infections in general, begins with washing your hands often.

## DEAL WITH IN-YOUR-FACE ISSUES.

While Mom knows that there are some things you can't control or have little control over, other things you can. We all need to be aware that first impressions are what people remember about us and, fair or not, they will mostly judge you first by what they see (or smell). While you can't always "cure" a malady the day that it occurs, you can work to prevent it from happening again.

## Bad Breath

Needless to say, bad breath is not the way to make a good first impression. Halitosis, as bad breath is known by in the medical profession, has a lot to do with the food you eat and the way you take care of your mouth. Foods with strong odors will linger in your mouth even after you have brushed your teeth and rinsed with mouthwash. Smoking and tobacco products do a number

on your breath, too. To help rid yourself of bad breath, have good oral hygiene: brush and floss at least twice a day, use mouthwashes, drink lots of water, don't smoke, and eat healthy foods. If all else fails, keep some mints in your pocket for close conversations.

## Acne

At one time or another, nearly every single person will suffer from a skirmish with acne. These inflamed skin blemishes are possibly some of the most hated things on the planet. Who hasn't had a "zit" at the worst possible time?! Well, in truth, acne can be a terrible problem to have, and some of us have a tougher time with it than others. When dealing with skin problems, it is important to realize that *you don't have acne because of anything that you have done, and it's really not because you didn't wash your face enough*. The causes are numerous, but the good news is that acne is treatable. If you are really suffering with acne, see a dermatologist. You deserve great looking skin!

## Warts

If you have warts, these little imperfections will most likely bother you more than those you meet. Warts are the result of viruses and often occur on our hands and feet. There are many treatments for eliminating warts. You will find some at your pharmacy, and others will require a visit to a dermatologist.

## Dandruff

This is a most annoying problem. White flakes on your shoulders when you are wearing a knock-out black dress can diminish the effect. Dandruff doesn't happen to you because you didn't wash your hair enough. It is just the flaking off of dead skin cells from your scalp and is a common problem for many people. Treatment for dandruff is simply to use shampoos that just might tingle a little. Mom recommends the ones containing tea tree oil. You can find them most anywhere.

## BEWARE OF STDS.

Mom wouldn't be doing anyone any favors if she didn't mention this touchy subject. Sexually transmitted diseases continue to be a huge problem in the United States. It seems no matter how much the subject is talked about, the numbers continue to rise. The ages of people that actually report STDs are between fifteen and twenty-four.

The frustrating thing about STDs is that they are easy to prevent! Of course, Mom recommends abstinence first and foremost. (If you play with fire, you might get burned, you know.) However, if you choose to be sexually active, please be safe. Use condoms, and don't take chances. You don't want to be counted in the next set of statistics. HIV/AIDS and human papillomavirus are terms too often heard in today's world. If you need more information on the subject, check out the Centers for Disease Control Web site at www.cdc.gov.

## AVOID DRUG AND ALCOHOL USE AND ABUSE.

Another touchy but necessary subject to discuss is drug and alcohol use or abuse. Many deaths and illnesses are caused every year by substance abuse. Too many good people die because they overindulge or they simply can't say no. Mom hopes that you use that good brain you've got and your common sense, but she also needs to make you aware of the pitfalls.

For years, the thought on alcohol use was this: moderation is best. That's a great line if you can stick to it. After all, alcohol is a drug, and long-term use of it will damage your liver, heart, and brain, and can cause serious stomach problems. Not to mention that alcohol use can change who you are, how you act, and how you react. I would guess that most everyone reading these words knows someone who has messed up his or her life or others' by abusing alcohol. Remember the moderation standard if you choose to drink.

Drug use of any kind is illegal. That is the bottom line. It doesn't matter if the drug is cocaine, marijuana, heroin, methamphetamine, or abused prescription or nonprescription drugs, they can be deadly. Drugs come in many different forms and can be taken and used in many different ways, but the end result is still the same: drugs are illegal, and they can kill you. Enough said.

## GET SMART ABOUT SMOKING AND TOBACCO USE.

Mom will need you to look up so that you can see her on her soapbox here. Tobacco is NOT good for you in any way, shape, or form. It is a nasty, disgusting, and expensive habit that you should never begin. However, if you have made the unfortunate decision to begin using tobacco products, there is good news for you. You can stop. It is never too late. You can save years of your life and your lung capacity by stopping today. It is your choice. Mom hopes you'll choose wisely.

## EAT WELL.

You can only drink so much beer and eat so much pizza at 2 a.m. After a while, your body will let you know that these habits are not such a good thing. Of course it's fun and an experience shared by many, but you do need to stop eating junk sooner rather than later.

Don't grab a Pop-Tart on the way out the door in the morning. Try a banana, apple, granola bar, or whole-grain muffin instead. Avoid fast food at lunch and dinner and go for the salads, veggies, fish, chicken, and leaner meats. Lay off the sodas, and drink a glass of water instead.

Eating habits are different for everyone, Mom knows. Our eating habits have a lot to do with how we grew up, but the present circumstances may also dictate what we eat. Just because money is tight doesn't mean you need to eat unhealthy foods.

Try to incorporate some good food choices into your everyday life. Choose fresh as often as possible. Changing the way you eat will not only decrease your waist size, it will improve your health and increase the length of your life!

## MAKE TIME TO EXERCISE.

Healthy eating won't do it all for you. Mom knows you need to get some exercise, too. If you adopt some healthy habits, including exercise, you will increase your energy level, and your life will improve in all areas.

Life is too short to sit around watching television and looking up thousands of things on your computer. Get off your butt and get moving. You'll have plenty of time to sit around when you are old. While you are young, get active, and soon your active new habits will become your lifestyle. For heaven's sake, just don't be lazy!

Join a gym, try yoga, take a dance class, go for a walk, start running, engage in a pick-up game of basketball, football, or soccer. You can get great exercise and blow

## TIPS FOR HEALTHY SLEEP

**Get adequate sleep.** For most people, eight hours will do it. However, you could need less or more.

**Settle into a regular sleeping schedule.** Try going to bed around the same time each night and getting up at the same time each morning.

**Get uninterrupted sleep.** In order for sleep to be rejuvenating, you should get it all in one time frame. Stay away from caffeine before bedtime.

**Make up that sleep loss.** Don't think you can sleep all day on Saturday to make up for missing a couple of hours a few nights a week. Try taking a twenty-to-thirty minute power nap during the day. It can be rejuvenating.

### Tips for BETTER sleep:

*Keep your bedroom dark, quiet, and cool.* Of course, this is the ideal sleeping situation for maximum benefit. A good-quality mattress and pillow can help, too. A cooler room also helps. Plus, it's just hard to sleep when it's hot.

*Eliminate stress.* Yeah right, you say. Okay, we're all stressed to some degree, but try to relax a little before bedtime. A warm bath or shower is helpful. Also, reading for pleasure, not work, can help ease you into a relaxed state before you turn off the lights and doze the night away.

off a little steam at the same time. Whatever physical activity you decide to try, embrace it and give it all you've got. Take good care of your body and keep it in good working order—it's the only one you get.

## GET PLENTY OF SLEEP.

Sleep is a necessity, not a luxury. If you don't get enough sleep, you can feel lethargic, experience drowsiness during the day, have reduced immunity to illnesses, have poor concentration and memory, and your productivity can be lowered. Wow, that's enough incentive for Mom to get some sleep, how about you? Sleep can help the quality of your life. It is a fact!

✛**Try taking multi-vitamins.** You might just find that you have a little more energy, and you won't get sick as often.

✛**Pick a Get-Healthy partner.** If you're having trouble getting motivated to diet or exercise, find somebody who will do it with you. The company and accountability factor helps a lot!

✛ **Wash up!** You can never overestimate the value of washing your hands for good health. So scrub away!

✛**Remember you've got good reason to be healthy!** The best reason to stay healthy and active is because you are worth it! This world needs people like you.

*Lack of activity destroys the good condition of every human being, while movement and methodical physical exercise save it and preserve it.*
**— PLATO**

*If your dog is fat, you aren't getting enough exercise.*
**— AUTHOR UNKNOWN**

# CHAPTER TWELVE

# It's All about Choices

*"Life's full of tough choices, isn't it?"*
**— URSULA THE SEA WITCH IN *THE LITTLE MERMAID***

The ball's in your court. It's all up to you. Your turn to decide. Make your move.

Are you breaking into a cold sweat yet? If so, Mom understands. After all, making choices can be a little overwhelming. Until this point in your life, your parents, in one way or another, ultimately decided pretty much everything. This isn't the case anymore. You are now in charge. You are now the boss of you.

Ain't it grand?

Not for everybody. While some of you have been itching to break free since you were nine and a half years old, other people will flip out when life hits them in the face. In fact, in the recent decades, more and more have decided they can't handle it, and they move back home with Mom and Dad. As Jerry Seinfeld says, "Not that there's anything wrong with that" . . . but we Moms have invested our energy trying to teach you how to stand on your own two feet. We've nudged you out of the nest, and gotten quite used to the extra room by now. So come on, it's time for you to test your wings and to see what's out there.

It's time for you to fly!

## First things first:
## Make intentional choices.

Every day for the rest of your life, you'll make hundreds of them—when (or if) to get up, what you're going to wear, who you're going to call, what you're going to eat . . . and those are just the easy ones!

Other choices in life are much more important than the size of your latte at Starbucks. And since you are the main one who must deal with the results of these decisions, you might as well make some good ones. Flying by the seat of your pants is not the best approach when it comes to life.

So go ahead, be *intentional*. Put some thought into your decisions, and do a lot of research. Don't make a completely random choice and regret it in two weeks. Write down what you want on paper. Make a list of all the options. List the pros and cons for any decision. Think it through and make your choices. Sure, you may regret it later (after all, hindsight's 20/20, and we can't know everything ahead of time). But at least you will be moving with a purpose, and hopefully headed in the general direction you want to go.

Here are a few pointers to get you in the right decisive frame of mind (and don't worry, following a little advice by no means diminishes your independence):

**#1 – You decide what you want.** Do you want to be close to friends and family, or would you rather be a good plane ride away? Do you want to live near the beach, or are the mountains more your style? Do you want to live in the city, or do you like life at a slower pace? Do you want a traditional life with work and family, or do you envision exotic jobs and trips? It is your life after all. Think about it.

**#2 – Go where you decide.** Move if you must. Find a safe place to live. Get a job. Make friends. Except for special circumstances, your boundaries are limited only by your dreams.

**#3 – Live your life.** You need to do what makes you happy and what you feel is right. Nike's slogan wasn't popular for nothing: just do it.

**MOM-*sense*:** When you get stuck and can't decide about something, one good way to clear your mind is to write a dividing line down half of a sheet of paper and list the pros of the decision on one side, and the cons on the other. The side that has the most reasons may just give you your answer!

## NEVER BE AFRAID OF CHANGE.

Because you are young and your life is fairly flexible, you have the perfect opportunity to experience all you can. This might mean moving to a new city or state, or maybe even to a new country. Settling in somewhere new, away from family and friends, can often lead to life-changing experiences and challenges that might not be possible if you stay where you are. Think outside the box, and be open to change.

Do a nationwide job search and see where it takes you. It could be exciting to take that job offer that has "some travel" included in the description. And when Mom says to travel and see sites while you are young, she knows what she is talking about. Once you settle down and start your own family, those opportunities tend to fade away. See the world while you still can, while it is fun, exciting, and adventurous. Seize the day! Before you know it, you'll have three kids and a mortgage.

**MOM-*sense*:** Don't ever move to another place because you are in love. That is, unless you really like the place and would be happy there even if your love drops you like a hot potato!

### TRY SOMETHING NEW, ESPECIALLY IF THE OLD ISN'T WORKING.

Keep your options open and be a flexible thinker. So things aren't going exactly the way you planned? Your job is boring, you make barely enough money to pay the rent and car note, and your friends aren't ready to grow up. Everyone has a realization about one or more of these things at some point in their life. Fortunately, change can be a good thing.

Look for another job, maybe even in a different field. Our original plans don't always work out, so take a step back and look at the bigger picture. You don't have to stay in a corporate job that takes more out of you than it pays. You can cut your losses, appreciate your lessons, and think again. You don't have to stay in a room filled with belligerent teenagers; look around at other options. This is the only life you're going to get. You can make it better, or you can sit and become stagnant where you are. Don't let years go by being unhappy because it's what's easiest. You do have a choice. You can change your situation.

### KNOW THAT TOUGH TIMES WILL HAPPEN.

Forrest Gump said it best when he simply said, "It happens." Well, you know what? It does happen. Sometimes, no matter how hard you are working, or how focused you are, or how organized you are, or how good you are at your job, tough times will come your way. It is inevitable.

There is a saying in the South that goes like this, "That which does not kill us makes us stronger." This line pops up at times when things seem to be the worst they can possibly be. But it is so true. Tough times strengthen our character and make better people of us all. Sometimes, it's only when we have to dig down deep that we find out how strong we can be. And if you feel like the trial you're going through is more than you can handle, remember another favorite phrase of mine: "This, too, shall pass."

It may be storming right now, but the sun will shine again. It always does. Hunker down, make the best of it, and stomp through some of those mud puddles if you can!

## OVERCOME YOUR BAD DECISIONS.

You may as well just face it; at some point in your life you will make a bad decision. Everyone does—that's how the phrase "learn from your mistakes" came to be. Sometimes it helps to evaluate why you made the bad decision: Was it made on the spur of the Moment, in a time of weakness, or because you had little (or wrong) information? But in the end, it doesn't help to agonize over it. What's done is done. When you make a bad decision, when you really screw up, the best thing you can do

is accept the consequences, make whatever restitution you can make, and move on (and remember that part about learning from it).

Most of all, don't allow yesterday's bad decision to influence today. Live in the present. Your actions following a bad decision are ultimately how you will be judged. And as for the people you can hardly face, in time they forget. It sometimes takes a while, but they do forget. Stand up straight, look people in the eye, and make a vow to yourself to be a better person today than you were yesterday. A little humility is good for the soul. And one day, when this humiliating time is a distant memory, you may have the opportunity to go a little easier on others when it's their turn to mess up big.

> *"Good judgment comes from experience. The problem is, a lot of experience comes from bad judgment."*
> — **COWBOY WISDOM**

## DON'T BE AFRAID TO ASK FOR ADVICE.

Okay. So you are independent and on your own, but some major decisions have got you stymied. It is perfectly okay to use your parents as a sounding board. More than likely, they have made some tough decisions in their lives and can understand your dilemma. They will possibly offer advice, which you do or do not have to take. Sometimes it just helps to have someone listen and be able to hear yourself talk it through.

If you are not comfortable discussing tough situations with your parents, there are other people you could turn to. Siblings, other family, friends, clergy, counselors, or even your boss can be a good choice to consult about life's decisions. There are always people in life who will listen if we have the courage to seek them out.

## LIVE A BALANCED LIFE.

If Mom had a Top-Ten-Words-of-Advice list, this one would be on it: "Live a balanced life." If you work all the time, you will become a bore. If you play all the time, you will become a slug. You will be a better person if you learn to balance all the facets of your life. It's really about being healthy—and that means more than hitting the gym five times a week. Being a healthy, whole person means you're investing some time and efforts in "feeding" your mental, physical, social, emotional, and spiritual self. Ignore any one of those components, and in time you'll feel off-kilter.

It is somewhat like juggling. You've got all these balls in the air, and you need to try to keep them up there. How do you do it? You give each one its proper amount of time and attention. Don't become a workaholic who does nothing else. But on the other hand, be the best employee you can be and give your job 100 percent when you are there. Likewise, have a great time with your friends doing things you enjoy, but remember you can only party and goof off so much. Eat healthy and exercise to keep strong and fit, but don't become obsessed with it.

You will probably go through periods where one or another aspect of your life takes too much of your energy and time, and after a while, you'll know it. Have you been ignoring relationships in pursuit of work? Have you been "hanging out" so much that you're losing your purpose and drive? Are hours in front of the television or computer numbing you life's larger concerns? Listen to that inner voice that says something's not right, and then ask yourself what's missing in your life. With a little insight and practice, you can find that sweet balance as you juggle along.

## DON'T TAKE ADVANTAGE OF OTHERS AND DON'T BE TAKEN ADVANTAGE OF.

Ah, another of Mom's pet peeves: people that take advantage of others. What a cowardly way to live. Unfortunately, there are too many over-grown bullies in this world, people who have nothing better to do than to look for people to gain something from. Don't be one of them. Earn what comes your way; don't wheedle it out of others. Mom taught you better than that.

On the other hand, don't let other people take advantage of you either. Now, I don't want you to go around being distrustful, but pay attention if you are always the one giving, lending, and going the extra mile. It is good to be kind and helpful to others, to give someone a lift, as they say. Just keep in mind that every once in a while, one of those passengers you're giving a lift to may be the one taking *you* for a ride.

## DON'T BE A GRUMP; HAVE A SENSE OF HUMOR.

Life is hard. And stressful, too. To make it, you must be a mature and fittingly serious grown-up person. But when that fails, it's time for a good guffaw. Don't take yourself too seriously—you're as human as the next person! Being able to laugh at situations you are in can put things into perspective. It is so easy to get bogged down in our day-to-day routines and become that person

> *A sense of humor . . . is needed armor. Joy in one's heart and some laughter on one's lips is a sign that the person deep down has a pretty good grasp on life.*
>
> **— HUGH SIDEY**

who worries and analyzes and schemes and plans to the point of being miserable. Sometimes, the best thing you can do is chuck it all (for a little while) and do whatever you can to relax and laugh a little.

It is so much better to laugh than to become angry and bitter. Whether it be calling that buddy who cracks you up, taking ballroom dancing with your fellow uncoordinated sister, or popping in reruns of *The Office* or *Seinfeld*, let yourself unwind sometimes. Go ahead, release some of those endorphins. You can be serious tomorrow.

## HELP SOMEONE ELSE: BECOME A VOLUNTEER.

If you have never volunteered for any type of charitable organization, you don't know what you're missing. It is definitely the most rewarding work you can do on this planet. Volunteering can help others so much, and it blesses you in the process. It's always a good choice to give of yourself to help another.

John Wesley, founder of the Methodist Church, had a motto that can be adopted by everyone: **Do all the good you can, by all the means you can, in all the ways you can, to all the people you can, as long as you ever can.**

If you want to volunteer but don't know where to start, try these Web sites as a launching pad:

**Volunteer Match** www.volunteermatch.org
**Global Volunteer Network** www.volunteer.org.nz
**Habitat for Humanity** www.habitat.org
**American Red Cross** www.redcross.org
**Network for Good** www.networkforgood.org
**Give.org**
**Charitynavigator.org**

Organizations always need donations, and by all means, donate if you have it to give. If you don't have the extra money to donate, seek out charities where you can spend time making a difference. There are so many groups that need dedicated workers, and who knows—one could be just around the corner from you. You can travel across the country, around the world, or down the street to do good.

*"Carry out a random act of kindness, with no expectation of reward, safe in the knowledge that one day someone might do the same for you."*

**— PRINCESS DIANA**

## DON'T EVER ASK ANYONE TO DO SOMETHING FOR YOU THAT YOU CAN DO YOURSELF.

Here is a little bit of Mom advice that actually comes from Mom's grandmother. *Never ask anyone to do something for you that you can do yourself.* Granny was a firm believer in taking care of oneself and all that encompasses. She was a tough girl who lived through the Great Depression and was accustomed to hard work and living without a lot of fluff.

Mom's advice to you is to never get so used to being pampered and spoiled that you can't or don't take care of yourself. Sure, we all need a helping hand now and then, but don't get attached to others' help; you need to feel the great satisfaction that comes with accomplishment. There's no reason to become lazy and complacent about the everyday tasks in your life. Jump up, get them done, and feel great about yourself and all that you have accomplished on your own with no help from anyone!

## DON'T LIVE A LIFE OF REGRET.

Woulda, shoulda, coulda . . . words to live by? Probably not. Often we go through life wishing we had done things differently. Everyone occasionally says, "I wish I had done . . ." or "I wonder what would have happened if . . ." but if you aren't careful, you can get stuck in the land of Looking Back.

Try to avoid the "if only's." For one thing, they inhabit a magical (and often) miserable world, and for another, you will never know what *would have happened if* . . . Chances are, if you'd lived *that* life you're dreaming of, you'd be sitting there wondering what life would be like if you'd lived *this* one. So take that old song that says, "if you can't be with the one you love, honey, love the one you're with!" and love the life you have now instead of the imaginary one you think you might have liked better.

*If you want happiness for an hour,*

*take a nap.*

*If you want happiness for a day,*

*go fishing.*

*If you want happiness for a year,*

*inherit a fortune.*

*If you want happiness for a lifetime,*

*help somebody.*

**— CHINESE PROVERB**

In the meantime, avoid future regrets by seizing today's opportunities. Often, circumstances like time, money, or relationships will dictate what you can do in your life, and you can't always squeeze it all in. If you hear yourself saying, *I wish I had done that,* get in the habit of adding, "Now, I will do this . . ." As for that golden gone-by opportunity? You may not have missed it anyway— perhaps it's just delayed a little.

## LEARN FROM THOSE AROUND YOU.

It's funny. With all the awards ceremonies I've either seen on television or read about or attended myself, I've never heard the recipient say, "Well, good thing I'm so smart. I got here all by myself, and I'm glad I had the brains to do it." No, whether the person is a super athlete, a talented actor, a savvy businessperson, or a Nobel prize winner, each one has a list of people to thank for helping them along their journey.

Mom hopes that, as you go through life, you will appreciate the lessons you can learn from those around you. Sure, the papers are filled with stories of lives gone wrong, but those are only half of the tale. Everywhere around you are people living good, honest, and remarkable lives. If you find yourself beating your head against the wall, consider asking someone a little older for a little advice. Read the words of people you admire throughout history. There's much to be gained from "standing on the shoulders of giants." And if all else fails, call Mom. I'm sure she'll have something to say about your situation.

## J.A.M. Session: Just one more thing . . .

◆ **Be ready to take responsibility.** A Moment will come when you will say, "CRAP (or something worse), my parents aren't going to get me out of this one!"

◆ **Grown up is as grown up does.** Being 21 does make you an adult, legally. But it doesn't always include maturity. That might just come along a little later.

◆ **Remember that patience is a virtue.** Learn to be patient. It takes time to find your way in the world.

*If you choose not to decide,*
*you still have made a choice.*
— **NEIL PEART**

## SOME CHOICE QUOTES ON LIVING A GOOD LIFE

Be a keeper of quotes. Jot them down in a favorite book or notebook, and refer to them often. Quotes are often words of wisdom that can be a trigger for us. (How do you think Mom got so smart?!)

*The doors we open and close each day decide the lives we live.*
**— FLORA WHITTEMORE**

*Your vision will become clear only when you look into your heart. He who looks outside, dreams. He who looks inside, awakens.*
**— CARL JUNG**

*It's a funny thing about life; if you refuse to accept anything but the best, you very often get it.*
**— SOMERSET MAUGHAM**

*We choose our joys and sorrows long before we experience them.*
**— KAHLIL GIBRAN**

*You are the person who has to decide.*
*Whether you'll do it or toss it aside;*
*You are the person who makes up your mind.*
*Whether you'll lead or will linger behind.*
*Whether you'll try for the goal that's afar.*
*Or just be contented to stay where you are.*
**— EDGAR A. GUEST**

# CHAPTER THIRTEEN

# Setting (and Keeping) Goals

*"Aim for nothing, and that's what you'll get."*

It's been said that knowing what you want in life is half the battle. You'd be surprised how many people go through life thinking so much about deadlines, schedules, and what they're going to wear the next day, that ten or twenty years pass before they remember to think about what they really want to do with their life.

Coming up with concrete goals for your life—and writing these goals down—helps get you where you want to be, one step at a time.

## First things first: Make lists of your goals.

Moms know that it is important to make lists. Of course, this is a part of being organized, which we talked about way back in Chapter 1, so I'm sure you're already there by now, aren't you?! Just in case you haven't got all your ducks in a row yet or your mp3 player was turned up too loud the first time, I'll share this tip one more time: it really helps to make a list of what you want. Whether it is a list of groceries to buy, calls to make, or dreams to pursue, writing those plans and goals down increases your commitment. Lists simply help get thoughts out of your head and into your life.

Sit down, get a paper and pen or your computer, and make a list. Turn off the TV and your cell phone and your iPod and your computer, and take some time to think long and hard about what you really want: Where do you want to go in your life? What do you want to see? What do you want to accomplish in your job/professional life? What are you looking for in your personal life? What steps can you take to get there?

Once you've taken the time to write out your goals, you are on your way—it may not be half the battle, but it's a mighty good start.

**MOM-*sense*:** Remember this quote I came across one day: "Goals that are not written down are just wishes."

# Set attainable goals.

After you have made your long-term list of goals, consider what you need to accomplish in the near future. Be sure that the goals you set for yourself are attainable. Don't sell yourself short, but be honest. In other words, set short-term goals that you can accomplish, and your success will help you move on to bigger and better things. For example, if you have gained some weight, don't say "I'm going to lose fifty pounds." Start smaller, like, "I'm going to exercise three days a week" or "I'm going to substitute low-fat crackers or carrots for potato chips." By breaking your ultimate goal into smaller, achievable pieces, you will ensure that you won't get discouraged before you even start.

The goals you have set for yourself need to evolve along with you. They should be just far enough away to keep you striving for them. By knowing what you want to achieve, you will know exactly where to concentrate all your efforts. You will even be aware of the distractions that can get you off course.

## THE GOAL LIST

*The Big Picture:
  25 Years or Lifetime Goals
*10 Years From Now
*5 Years Down The Road
*1 Year Plan
*6 Months Out
*1 Month

**MOM-*sense*:** Each time, make your goals progressively smaller so that you can reach those lifetime goals. Make sure that you base each one on the previous plan. Include these in your list: Education, Family, Career, Physical, Financial, and Pleasure. Make sure that your goals reflect your thoughts and not those of your parents or friends.

## BE POSITIVE AND HAVE A GOOD ATTITUDE.

Of course, reaching your goals will be much easier if you approach everything with a positive outlook and a good attitude. A bad attitude can cost you success, as well as friendships, along the way. Think about it—what would Wilbur and Orville Wright, Michael Jordan, Tiger Woods, Oprah, or Bill Gates have accomplished without a positive attitude? History books are filled with people who met failure after failure, yet refused to give up—Christopher Columbus, Abraham Lincoln, and Rosa Parks, to name a few. In the same way, the potential for you to succeed increases tremendously when you have a good attitude.

## USE VISUALIZATION AND POSITIVE SELF-TALK.

If you are a visual person (and even if you aren't, it's worth a try), practice visualizing yourself finding success at that skill, job, or relationship you've been striving toward. Take time out of each day to sit quietly, close your eyes, and "see" yourself performing the task successfully. Habitually using this technique has helped successful business people, professional athletes, and high achievers of all kinds improve their performance and reach their goals.

Also remember that what you say to yourself matters. It's hard to get that promotion or tackle that chore you've been avoiding if your mind keeps saying things like, "I'll never be good enough" or "I can't do it." Retrain your brain by intentionally saying positive statements about your areas of weakness—hey, you can even post sticky notes all over your mirror and refrigerator. After reading and saying, "I am competent, I can have discipline in my eating habits" over and over, you may just start believing it! You've heard it said, "What the mind can conceive, it can achieve." So, go ahead, trick your mind into thinking you can do it!

## ACE JOB INTERVIEWS.

The time has come for you to go on a job interview. Don't get all stressed out about it. Just prepare yourself and take steps to make a good impression. You want the job, and

## TIPS FOR SUCCESSFUL JOB INTERVIEWS

★ Keep your resumé up to date and saved on your computer. Include your educational background, work experience, and dates. (Make sure you or a friend proofreads it.)

★ Dress appropriately for the job. Jeans may be okay at a pizza parlor, but not in an office building where everyone wears a suit.

★ Be on time; forget that—arrive early.

★ Smile and be cordial from the time you arrive, until you leave.

★ Shake hands (firmly, of course!) as you introduce yourself.

★ Sit down after the interviewer suggests you do so.

★ If someone new is introduced to you, stand up and shake their hand.

★ Say "Thank You" to the interviewer for taking the time to see you.

★ Speak clearly, answer questions honestly, and look the person in the eye.

★ Don't be afraid to talk about your achievements and abilities that will help you succeed in this job.

★ Ask questions about the company and the position for which you are applying.

your task is to make sure that they *need* you for the job. It's time to sell yourself, and do a bang-up job of it.

### WORK HARD.

Mom always says to work hard. But what she really means is don't just work hard, be good at your job as well. You may feel as though you are not working at a job that is ideal for you. That doesn't matter. What does matter is that you do it well. It could very well be a stepping stone for a fabulous job down the road. If you choose not to do your best or give it all you've got, then don't expect a glowing recommendation for the next opportunity . . .

Always treat your job as though it is very important. Be a team player and think in terms of "we," not "I." Be effective and efficient. Be on time and always dress appropriately. Work extra hours if you need to. Be proactive and ask questions; don't sit around doing nothing. The bottom line is to try to enjoy the job you do have and learn from it what you can. Your goal is to look back on it one day from a job you like much better.

## TREAT SCHOOL LIKE YOUR JOB.

So perhaps you're a college student, and that is fantastic. Right now you may be living on your own, with no parents' rules, and staying out all night going to parties . . . but you still must go to class. Yes, class does come first. Remember why your parents sent you to college in the first place.

Of course you should have a good time while you are in college. No one expects you to sit home every night. However, you are expected to get yourself up, go to class, take notes, study, and do the best you can.

If you find yourself doing poorly in a particular class, make an appointment, with your professor. Those hours posted on his door are for a reason; he or she is available for help. Be on time for your appointment and be very clear when you speak. You must make the effort, because the professor is not going to come knock on your door and find you. Remember, you are an adult and need to handle the responsibilities that come with freedom. How you perform in school is part of what helps you reach the goals you have set for your life.

## NEVER BE AFRAID TO DREAM.

As you're being responsible and pursuing your goals, remember you're allowed to dream. Dreams can be as big or as small as you wish, and dreams don't always have to be realistic. Never forget that—*plans* that you make are realistic, not dreams. Dreams are in our lives to allow us some Moments of escape, to add fun and a little spice. No one can tell you what you can dream, and you are not required to share your dreams with anyone unless you choose.

Every one has the right to dream; we all need to believe in the improbable at times. So go ahead, let yourself imagine that one day you'll actually win that lottery or marry that girl or make that professional team. And as you enjoy your fantasy, remember that, just as Cinderella sings, every now and then dreams do come true.

## GAIN KNOWLEDGE FROM MANY SOURCES.

Moms know that successful people in life seem to share a love of learning. Never content that they know it all or have "figured everything out," they are willing to put themselves in vulnerable, new situations and stretch their minds and capabilities.

## Be a Lifelong Learner:
## Read, read, and read some more.

Remember how exciting it was when you were first learning to read? You began to learn so much so quickly, and you devoured the written word. Well, guess what? You can still learn a ton by reading. Read everything you can get your hands on—newspapers, magazines, and books; fiction and non-fiction. All the information you absorb will only improve the person you already are.

## Improve your vocabulary.

Knowledge of words and their meanings is such a great thing to have. A great way to improve your vocabulary is by doing crossword puzzles. You'll be surprised just how much they will expand your vocabulary. And once again, probably the best way to learn new words is to read, read, read! The more words you know will help you to make better choices when writing or speaking to others.

## Meet as many people as you can.

You don't have to be best friends with them all, but you can certainly benefit from knowing as many people as possible. And be open to meeting people outside of your normal social group, age level, and background. You will learn so much from people from different walks of life. And you never know when you will need a recommendation from someone or a great tip on a job opening.

## Be a detective, of sorts.

Be a seeker of information. If you are interested in a subject and you know little about it, don't let that keep you from becoming an expert. Ask questions, do research, and learn all you can. Use multiple sources, including the Internet, books, magazines, and other people.

## Don't let failure
## get you down.

There's always the chance that you won't succeed at one of your goals. Everyone experiences failure at something during his or her lifetime. As coaches sometimes tell their teams after a loss, "You can't win them all." If you don't succeed at reaching one of your goals, it doesn't mean that you are a failure. It means you failed at something. There is a big difference.

It is a good idea to consider a failure as an isolated incident. You can't let one solitary event distort your view of achieving success after this. Successful people that are high achievers don't let individual failures get them down. They know an important secret about life: the only true failure is giving up.

＊**Have good posture.** People will look up to you if your back is straight and you are standing tall. Your presence is always noted if your posture is good.

＊**Add some flair.** Use cream-colored paper when you print your resumé. It will stand out from all the other white ones.

＊**Do some goal-reading.** If you want some more information on setting goals, and tracking and keeping them, you're in luck. The books on this subject are endless.

＊**Enjoy the journey.** Don't get so focused on "performing well" and reaching your goals that you can't relax and have fun. Have a good sense of humor as you try, fail, and try again.

*The most important thing about goals is having one.*
— GEOFFRY F. ABERT

# CHAPTER FOURTEEN

# Remember Who You Are and Where You Came From

*"A good name is worth more than riches."*
**— PROVERBS 22:1**

I bet that many of you heard some version of this chapter's title several times while growing up. Mom may have said, "Remember who you are and where you came from!" when you went on your first out-of-town trip back in junior high. Dad may have barked out, "Remember you're a (fill in your last name). And (fill in your last name)'s know how to behave" when you went off to college.

You may have barely heard your parents' advice as you headed out the door with your friends. But I imagine that somewhere inside, you knew what they meant. Those words, in essence, are a summary of many things your Mom and Dad wanted to remind you about—things they've been telling you for years: Remember your manners. Don't slouch. Be careful who your friends are. Keep your nose clean. Stand up straight. Be considerate. Always tell the truth. The list was too long to repeat. And you wouldn't have listened anyway. It's simply easier to use the one-liner.

Yes, "Remember who you are and where you came from" is a token line, one that says, Hey—while you're out there having fun in the big world, try not to forget all the things we tried to teach you; don't embarrass us, but more than that, be proud of who you are and true to what you know is right.

Trust me, this line will never go out of style or use. It's a token line, alright. A token line straight from your parents' hearts.

## First things first: Remember your values.

Old-fashioned values still have a place in today's fast-paced world. Doing the "right thing" is not a relic of the past. Honor, trust, reliability, loyalty, pride, dependability, support, and strength are exhibited in lives all across this land everyday, and they all have a place in your life. Being a person with values doesn't make you a stick-in-the-mud or a goody-two-shoes. And even if it does, who cares? Anyone can "go with the flow" and follow the latest craze or habit. It takes a person of value to have values.

Mom knows you're going to stretch your wings out on your own. You'll grow and change; you may acquire a new accent, adopt a new style, and even get a new (and weird, I might add) haircut. But as you navigate the twists and turns of your life, and experience new things, don't let go of your foundation. Guard your integrity. Be a person who sticks by a friend in troubled times. Be a person who does the right thing and who does it because it is the right thing to do. Keeping your word, keeping your promises, keeping your faith in others are all qualities that endure. As my grandmother once told me, "Keep your values and your values will keep you."

## EMBRACE YOUR MORALS.

I'm afraid the word *morals* gets a bad rap sometimes. What words come to mind when you think about morals? How about some of these: decent, ethical, honorable, respectable, trustworthy, and truthful? Now for a different question: Do any of these words describe you? I'll bet they do. You don't have to be labeled a "saint" to have good morals.

Morals are a part of your being, your core. All the good things you were taught in your life either by your parents or someone else are inside you and are still a huge part of who you are. Of course, we all stray a bit from time to time and sometimes end up miles away from where we started. But, you know what the truth is? 99.9 percent of the time we circle back around and become the very people our parents raised us to be. We may not be exactly what Mom and Dad envisioned, but usually, we're pretty darn close.

## STRIVE FOR INTEGRITY, CHARACTER, AND A GOOD REPUTATION.

Wow, could any three words say more about you than *integrity, character,* and *reputation*? The definitions of these words often overlap with each other. For example, *integrity* is the soundness of moral *character*; *character* is a person of good *reputation*; and *reputation* is *character* in the public's estimation. Even though there are similarities, integrity, character, and reputation should not be confused with one another.

**Integrity** is the basis for the other qualities to be built upon. It is "doing the right thing when no one is looking." You maintain your integrity by being true even in little things as you go through your life. Integrity is you knowing what you stand for and then sticking to those principles. You will have to make some tough choices in life, but if you have integrity, your actions will match your core beliefs.

## TRAITS OF A PERSON OF INTEGRITY

✛ Chooses honesty and fairness over personal gain and "shortcuts"

✛ Serves others instead of seeking power

✛ Does what he/she believes is right, with or without an audience

✛ Always puts in an honest day's work (doesn't cheat others of time or effort)

✛ Is the same person in every circumstance (doesn't change to suit others)

✛ Lives out core principles daily or "practices what he/she preaches"

**Character** is the combination of moral qualities, ethical standards, and principles that make up who you are. Character is established in you by the way you deal with the

*Character is much easier kept, than recovered.*

**— THOMAS PAINE**

changing circumstances of life. Your true character is especially revealed in times of crisis and difficulty. If you always fall apart or lose it when things don't go your way, or if you do the right thing "except when people pressure you," your character needs some work! Good character requires that you do the right thing even if it is risky or costly. Always remember that your character is defined both by what you say and don't say, and what you do and don't do. And, you should know that what *you* do can and does make a difference.

**Reputation**, of course, is how other people see you. A good reputation is often referred to as "having a good name." In truth, you will only have a good reputation when you are a person of good character. So the good news is, if you're doing what you should be, you don't have to worry about this one—by maintaining your integrity and character, then your reputation will happen all by itself.

## RESPECT YOUR FAMILY.

What would we do without our families, the people we love—and love to argue with? Truthfully, you never know what you'd do without them until you have spent a significant amount of time away. The old line *absence makes the heart grow fonder* usually proves true with our families.

> Families are like fudge—mostly sweet with a few nuts.
> — AUTHOR UNKNOWN

When you are out on your own with all your responsibilities, you may begin to miss your family. More than anything, you will learn to appreciate all the things they did for you. (Taking out your trash, cooking your own meals, and paying your own bills does wonders for making you miss Mom and Dad!) You'll probably still think your parents are old and your siblings are weird or spoiled (don't we all?). But, you will hopefully find some common ground and reach a level of understanding and mutual appreciation, no matter how good or bad things were before you went out on your own. All families have some level of dysfunction, but no matter what, they are *your family*—the people who have known you your whole life. They've seen you win, lose, laugh, cry, gripe, burp, eat, sleep, and go through your awkward phase. And they're still in your corner all the same.

Someday you will have a family of your own, but for now you are still a part of your first family. Enjoy the

"The family. We were a strange little band of characters trudging through life sharing diseases and toothpaste, coveting one another's desserts, hiding shampoo, borrowing money, locking each other out of our rooms, inflicting pain and kissing it to heal in the same instant, loving, laughing, defending, and trying to figure out the common thread that bound us all together."

**— ERMA BOMBECK**

**MOM-*sense*:** If you aren't a person who "calls home all the time," consider picking out one time a week, say Sunday night, to call your Mom or Dad and check in. It's a simple gesture that helps you stay connected.

time you get to spend with them, whether it is a lot or not so much. You will probably never change them, so choose to enjoy them instead. Laugh, smile, reminisce, fight, cry, hug, love, and forgive them, because they won't be around forever. And they do the same for you.

**REMEMBER YOUR MANNERS.**
No matter how old, important, or cool you become, saying "please" and "thank you" is never out of place. It is a common courtesy to fellow human beings who are likely doing the best they can with what

they have. If you are too busy and high and mighty to show simple kindness to both strangers and loved ones, then you have lost more than you've gained on your climb up the ladder to success.

Just take the time to be nice. Even to the clerk in the checkout line. You never know how a simple smile or a kind word will bless someone.

And while I'm on manners, don't give someone a limp hand when you shake hands. You've probably had someone do it to you. It feels like their hand might just fall off in yours. Give a good firm handshake and people will remember you. Once, I met Ann Curry of *The Today Show;* she may be a thin, lovely lady, but let me tell you, she has one firm handshake. She was almost apologetic and told me that people always tell her that her handshake is too firm. Nevertheless, I'll always remember Ann because of her handshake.

Last but not least on this subject, one of Mom's pet peeves: people who will not look you in the eye when you talk to them are so very rude. Please don't join their ranks! You are no longer a young teenager with a need to roll your eyes back in your head when someone speaks to you. Look people in the eye and let them know they have your full attention. It's a compliment to the other person and a show of honesty for someone to look another in the eye while having a conversation. It will also pay off for you because you'll be known as a stand-up person with a firm handshake who looks people in the eye. (If you ever run for president, you're halfway there!)

## BE A GOOD FRIEND.

Once again, the old saying is true: to have a friend, you must be a friend. And since you're going to be some type of friend anyway, you might as well be a good one.

> Friends are relatives you make for yourself.
> — EUSTACHE DESCHAMPS

Being a real friend to someone requires time, attention, and intent. You must be loyal and honest, sympathetic and forgiving, supportive and able to give and take. I'm sure you agree with Mom that although being a truly good friend is an awesome responsibility, it is truly worth the effort.

> A friend is one of the nicest things you can have and one of the best things you can be.
> — DOUGLAS PAGELS

## TAKE RESPONSIBILITY SERIOUSLY.

So you've had a great time during your school years. You enjoyed all the perks of having the parents pay for your life up until now, and you had a lot of fun and goofed off maybe more than you should have. But now it's time to get serious. Time to get a "real" job and begin the journey of becoming the self-supporting, responsibility-taking you. (And if you're just starting college or somewhere in between living under your folks' roof and being fully on your own, it's a good time to practice independent and responsible living.) Mom loves you, Kid, but it's time to cut off those apron strings!

You are an adult now. Mom is not going to be there to wake you up in the morning or to come back again after you hit the snooze bar for the sixth time. She's not going to be there to cook well-balanced meals for you and make sure that you eat right. She won't even be there to turn off the lights and the TV and to lock the door when you forget. It is all up to you now. Are you up to the challenge?

Taking on responsibility for oneself is a little scary sometimes, but take heart, you've been preparing for this all your life. That is, you have been if you paid attention. If not, then you'll be making a few mistakes. Oh heck, you'll make mistakes anyway, everyone does. When you make them, admit it, try to rectify it, and move on.

Being a responsible person is way more than just getting a job and paying your bills on time. Responsibility shows in the way you treat people, the times you arrive (and leave), the way you spend your money, and the way you treat your body. If you start to look at everything you've got to do (pay the utilities, register your car tags, plan and shop for meals, earn a living, floss, write your senator . . .), it can get overwhelming. So take it one day at a time. Have a plan for tomorrow, but concentrate on what can be done today. Sure, you're going to decorate a house one day, host a Thanksgiving meal, and get your kid through college, but don't worry about all that now. If you take your responsibilities seriously, things will work out for you (and once again, your Mom will be so proud!).

---

**A responsible person is . . .**

**S**table
**T**rustworthy
**R**eliable
**O**n-time
**N**ever negligent
**G**iving Back

---

## RESERVE A PLACE FOR SPIRITUALITY, RELIGION, AND FAITH.

Though all of us must wrestle with life's deepest questions in the privacy of our hearts and minds, Mom has found it sure helps to have a group of people who can encourage you along the journey. A faith-based community is a good place to find such people.

Most religions offer a path for you to deepen your relationship with God. In your search for that path, don't dive into a new, unfamiliar faith group too quickly. No matter what your belief system is, you should educate yourself about the practices, traditions, liturgy and customs of your choice of faith. In short, do a little research. Most churches, fellowships, mosques, and temples welcome visitors, so take this time in your life to attend some different congregations; observe the services they offer and the message they preach. Make a point to talk to the people who are members there to see if you share similar ideas and beliefs. (Most folks are not shy about sharing their beliefs if you are interested.) Some places even offer classes for new attendees to learn about the church's beliefs and traditions. Taking full advantage of these opportunities will better equip you as you seek out a place of worship to call "home."

Once you find a place that appeals to you and shares your basic core beliefs, go ahead and get more involved to see if you really "fit" with that particular group of followers. If it takes you a while to find a place that feels comfortable and right, that's okay. Faith is not an exact science, and it is okay to question.

One more thing—while you may be inclined to take a different route than the one you were raised with or that your parents chose, the beliefs you were taught as a child are still a part of you. You may find that they resurface when life gets tough, circumstances change, or life events trigger family memories. Accept that your faith heritage is a part of you, and that knowing this, you are free to forge your own unique faith walk. You can choose your own path.

## WAYS TO STRENGTHEN YOUR FAITH

✓ Attend a regular service or gathering weekly.
✓ Develop a habit of having a quiet time of reading and meditating on spiritual topics and texts.
✓ Educate yourself about the practices, beliefs, and customs of a faith-based fellowship.
✓ Acquaint yourself with others who share similar beliefs.
✓ Be thankful.
✓ Serve others.
✓ Pray often.

## BE ACCEPTING AND RESPECTFUL OF OTHERS.

One quick trip to the mall can remind you that the world is full of all kinds of people. We are different colors. We speak different languages. We dress differently. We have different customs and rituals. We have different religions. We have different incomes. Heck, we even have different ring-tones. But, we all have one thing in common—we are all human beings.

**There are also other things we have in common.** We have families. We have dreams. We have failures. We have successes. We have regrets. We have forgiveness in our hearts. We have love in our hearts. Pick out someone who seems to be completely opposite of you, and remember this truth: we humans are more alike than we are different.

Do not let the negativity in the world cloud your perspective of others. We are equal on the most basic of fields: our humanity. Be a person who is capable of seeing past the outer differences. Remember that everyone deserves to be accepted and respected—even that annoying lady in traffic, that "punk" racing through the parking lot, or that slow man in the check-out line. More importantly, no one deserves to be the target of hatred, discrimination, or ridicule. You be the person who breaks down barriers. When you behave in a positive way, maybe someone else will notice and the cycle of good will continue. At least, that's what Mom hopes.

## BE PATRIOTIC AND LOVE YOUR COUNTRY.

*Excuse me for a minute while I get out my soapbox . . . okay, there, I'm on it. Now listen:* It doesn't matter what your political affiliation is or whether you agree with the politicians in office. For our country and its communities, towns, and cities to be strong, we must all be united in one thing: our commitment to America and appreciation for all we've been given.

Sure, we're not perfect! Sure we've got corruption and crime and taxes and more problems than you can fit on a CNN broadcast. But do you know how many people in the world would give everything to have what we do? I learned so much from my Grandfather, who served in World War II, about patriotism and respect for the people who volunteer to protect our country. So often we forget how many people have died so that we can enjoy the freedoms we take for granted every day.

Fly an American flag on holidays— or every day. Be a proud *American*, not a disgruntled Democrat or Republican. Being patriotic doesn't show an alliance with any one group. Being patriotic shows pride in your country, concern for your fellow citizens, and respect for all of those who have gone before. Being patriotic shows you care about our nation's future.

## VOTE.

And listen (*adjusting soapbox*), don't ever miss an opportunity to vote in an election. The day you were born, you inherited the right as a free American to vote and choose. Now, having said that, your vote may not always count toward the winning outcome of an election. But don't let that discourage you from participating in the process. Always make the time to vote. It's your privilege as a citizen.

## WRITE THANK YOU NOTES.

No, it has not gone out of style. And, *double no*, a "thank you email" is *not* sufficient. I hate to get all generational on you, but it's true, younger people are just plain lazy about thank you notes! You do not need to have monogrammed stationery in order to write a heartfelt thank you note; you do not have to write a tear-evoking remarkable piece of literature. All you have to do is quit making excuses and sit down and write the darn thing. Not only does writing a thank you note take just a Moment (a fraction of the time and thought that your note recipient invested in you), it is absolutely the courteous and respectful thing to

do. Being grateful is good for the soul. And sitting down and giving up the few minutes it takes to hand-write someone a note of thanks is probably one of the best habits you can acquire in your life.

So, please, honey, be a thankful person and write a note. You'll be glad you did.

**MOM-*sense*:** Send a thank you note within one week of receiving a gift, favor, or kind gesture from someone. If you don't get it done in a week, do it later anyway. When you write the note, include briefly a line about the gift or the occasion on which it was given. Just write words that you would say if the person was standing in front of you. A personal touch is more meaningful.

## GIVE SOMETHING BACK: LEAVE THIS WORLD BETTER THAN YOU FOUND IT.

Get involved in some organization that does good. Become a volunteer, be a mentor, help build a house, buy and donate school supplies, be a tutor, feed hungry people, read to sick children, help plant a garden, and by all means, donate clothes you don't wear to people who can use them. Be a difference maker, not a person who says, "I'd really like to help, but I don't know what to do." Find a way to make a difference. Get involved, roll up your sleeves, and get your hands dirty.

By the way, every single day we hear that we should "save our planet." You may not be able to stop pollution and reduce global warming single-handedly, but you can certainly do your part by cleaning up after yourself. Don't *ever* litter, and always pick up garbage when you see it. (It needs to be picked up by someone—might as well be you.) Walk somewhere instead of driving, recycle when possible, use less energy, and try to improve the quality of life for you and everyone around you. Your children will thank you someday. *(Or maybe they won't, but wouldn't you rather them be living with fresh air and plenty of natural resources anyway?)*

### LAST, BUT NOT LEAST, CALL YOUR MOTHER!

Oh, and it's okay to call your Dad, too. These two people love you more than anyone ever will. It's safe for me to say this because I know it is true. You'll know it too someday when you have children of your own.

It doesn't matter that you are grown up, living on your own, and think you know more than they do. If they did a good job raising you, then tell them about it. If they didn't do such a good job in some areas, forgive them. They did the best they could, and surely you realize that now that you are an adult.

So, go ahead, call your parents! Call just to say, "I love you," or "I miss you," or "Happy Mother's Day" or "I don't know how to get this ink stain out of my pants." (You can also call to ask for money—just pretend there are other reasons, too.) Your parents will happily listen to all the exciting, frustrating, mundane details of your life—they've had good practice—so give them the chance . . .
*Make that call!*

## J.A.M. Session:
## Just one more thing . . .

❖ **Dot your i's.** When you send someone a handwritten note, be absolutely sure you spelled the person's name correctly.

❖ **Do it right the first time.** Something worth doing is worth doing right. (It probably won't be easy either.)

❖ **Practice random acts of kindness.** It's not just a saying; it's a lifestyle.

❖ **Forgive.** All of us are human (even Mom) and will mess up again and again. Holding grudges only gives you a sour expression and indigestion or high blood pressure. Forgiveness is the best way—both for others and yourself.

I leave you with one of my favorite poems that was also a favorite of a very special mother, Mother Teresa . . .

*People are often unreasonable, illogical,*
*and self-centered;*
**Forgive them anyway.**
*If you are kind, people may accuse you*
*of selfish, ulterior motives;*
**Be kind anyway.**
*If you are successful, you will win some*
*false friends and some true enemies;*
**Succeed anyway.**
*If you are honest and frank,*
*people may cheat you;*
**Be honest and frank anyway.**
*What you spend years building,*
*someone could destroy overnight;*
**Build anyway.**
*If you find serenity and happiness,*
*they may be jealous;*
**Be happy anyway.**
*The good you do today, people will often*
*forget tomorrow;*
**Do good anyway.**
*Give the world the best you have, and it*
*may never be enough;*
**Give the world the best you have anyway.**
*You see, in the final analysis, it is between*
*you and God;*
**It was never between you and them anyway.**